THE
CLIMBING
HANDBOOK

STEVE LONG

A FIREFLY BOOK

Published by Firefly Books Ltd. 2007

Copyright © 2007 Marshall Editions

First printing

Publisher Cataloging-in-Publication Data (U.S.)

Long, Steve.
    The climbing handbook : the complete guide to safe and exciting rock climbing / Steve Long.
[192] p. : col. ill., photos. ; cm.
Includes index.
Summary: Summary: Introduction to climbing, including equipment, techniques, and places to climb.
ISBN-13: 978-1-55407-278-1 (pbk.)
ISBN-10: 1-55407-278-6 (pbk.)
1. Rock climbing. I. Title.
796.5223 dc22   GV200.2.L664 2007

Library and Archives Canada Cataloguing in Publication

Long, Steve, 1959-
    The climbing handbook : the complete guide to safe and exciting rock climbing / Steve Long. — 1st ed.
Includes bibliographical references and index.
ISBN-13: 978-1-55407-278-1
ISBN-10: 1-55407-278-6
    1. Rock climbing. I. Title.
GV200.2.L67 2007   796.522'3
C2006-906921-2

Published in the United States by
Firefly Books (U.S.) Inc.
P.O. Box 1338, Ellicott Station
Buffalo, New York 14205

Published in Canada by
Firefly Books Ltd.
66 Leek Crescent
Richmond Hill, Ontario L4B 1H1

Conceived, edited and designed in the United Kingdom by
Marshall Editions
The Old Brewery
6 Blundell Street
London N7 9BH
www.quarto.com

Publisher: Richard Green
Commissioning editor: Claudia Martin
Art direction: Ivo Marloh
Project editor: Johanna Geary
Editorial and design: Seagull Design
Production: Anna Pauletti

Dedicated to Sion Idwal Long

Previous page: Climbing Motörhead, Eldorado, Grimsel Pass, Swizerland
This page: Rappelling at Thaiwand Wall Towers, Thailand

Originated in Hong Kong by Modern Age
Printed in China by Midas Printing
International Limited

THE
CLIMBING
HANDBOOK

The complete guide to safe and exciting rock climbing

STEVE LONG

CONTENTS

INTRODUCTION

Climbing is truly a "sport for life." Exciting days spent hanging above breathtakingly beautiful vistas, vacations in tropical paradises, mountain adventures, the social camaraderie of a team solving a difficult sequence of moves up a time-sculpted boulder, or scaling an urban artificial wall; all guarantee days to savor, no matter what your age or ability.

Climbing can be enjoyed as an occasional diversion, or as a commitment to athletic endeavors, demanding regular training and practice; it can be a hobby or a way of life. Some climbers succeed in building a successful career from their passion; others earn just enough to fund the latest adventure. Like all adventure sports, climbing can be addictive.

Gravity is an ever-present companion for climbers and at times it can be an enemy. Any introduction to this sport must carry a caveat: climbing is a hazardous activity with attendant risks of falling or impact from falling rocks. Part of the attraction comes from learning how to manage these risks and feeling in control perched above an intimidating void, but even the most experienced climber can suffer an accident or make a careless mistake. Never take your safety for granted, and always accept well-meant advice with good grace—it could save your life one day.

Despite—or maybe because of—the obvious dangers, climbers are neither foolhardy nor reckless, however much the popular press would have us believe. Rock climbing is certainly much less hazardous than driving a car and the rewards are far greater.

Using this book

This book is designed to help both novices and experienced climbers gain the skills and knowledge required to participate safely in some or all of the thrilling activities known collectively as rock climbing.

Most sections are laid out in self-contained double-page spreads that can be read in sequence or as the mood strikes you.

The opening sections describe the main variations of the sport, and the equipment, safety and movement skills required to enjoy them. After a thorough grounding we take a look at basic and advanced training methods, with tips from some top coaches and performers.

The second half of the book opens with practical tips on avoiding problems and a basic set of skills for dealing with difficult situations or injuries. After an introduction to advanced and more committing forms of climbing we take a lightning tour around the world's best climbing destinations and conclude with some advice for anybody hoping to embark on a career in this fulfilling sport.

A climber in the mythical landscape of **Meteora**. These massive rock towers near Kalambaka, Greece, are dotted with ancient monasteries perched on the edge of cliffs hundreds of feet above ground (Meteora means "suspended in the air").

HISTORY OF CLIMBING

Ancient origins

The origins of rock climbing as we know it today are shrouded in mystery. We know that for centuries climbers have ventured into precipitous territories: the medieval monasteries of Meteora in northern Greece, stone passageways as far afield as the Wadi Rum in Jordan, and Ladakh in Tibet bear silent testimony to journeys that wove through sheer rock walls and canyons. Interest in the mountains has generally reflected the spirit of the age; the remarkable first ascent of France's Mont Aiguille in 1492 was made by mercenaries for the king's glory.

The Victorian mountaineers

As the Age of Discovery merged with the Romantic Movement, the Victorians brought a robust mixture of pragmatism and idealism that was increasingly manifested in adventurous bids to gain elusive summits. In the United Kingdom early scrambling forays characterized this period. The first milestones have been variously attributed to poet Samuel Coleridge's descent of Broad Stand on Scafell Pike in the English Lake District (1802), or his

colleague William Wordsworth's bird-nesting escapades. The botanically motivated ascent by the Reverends Williams and Bingley of the East Terrace of Clogwyn du'r Arddu in North Wales in 1798 is often cited as the first real rock climb. Many other scrambles soon followed; significant feats included the first ascent of Pillar Rock in Lakeland in the English Lake District in 1826 and the West Buttress of Lliwedd, in Snowdonia, North Wales, climbed in 1883. There are accounts of bouldering ascents at Fontainebleau near Paris dating from 1874 onward. This was of course the "Golden Age of Alpinism": rock-climbing skill was an essential prerequisite for success on many of the peaks ascended during the 19th century, epitomized by the ascent and eventful descent of the Matterhorn in 1865.

The sport of rock climbing

Britain's Walter Parry Haskett Smith is regarded by many historians as the "father of rock climbing," principally for his famous solo ascent of Napes Needle on Great Gable in the English Lake District. However, his achievements were eclipsed by events in East Germany, where the elimination of "aid" points in Saxony was already actively pursued. Another Brit, Owen Glynne Jones, pushed standards toward the end of the 19th century, but World War I brought an end to play shortly after the success of Germans Siegfried Herford and George S. Sansom in forcing their way up Scafell's Central Buttress, with the judicious use of a shoulder as a foothold, known as "combined tactics." This technique was also accepted practice in Saxony, where the American Oliver Perry-Smith and his German companion Rudolf Fehrmann arguably tackled even harder climbs.

Women have always participated in rock climbing, often at the highest levels. Here, 12-year-old **Irene Jackson** tackles a mountain route on Dow Crag in the English Lake District in 1933.

This teamwork approach to overcoming a short, hard step was a typical strategy known as "combined tactics." By the time this photograph was taken in the White Mountains, U.S., in 1945, the free-climbing tradition had largely rejected this as a legitimate technique.

Postwar years

Climbing was now an established sport around the world. John Salathé's 1947 ascent of Yosemite's Lost Arrow and then Sentinel Rock in 1950 brought the U.S. sharply into the modern era. British standards were raised by the legendary emergence of Joe Brown and Don Whillans, whose first ascents consolidated a new era of social change. Italian Walter Bonatti achieved perhaps the finest solo rock climb of all time with his six-day first ascent of the SW Pillar of the Petit Dru (Chamonix) in 1955. The floodgates had opened. Americans Royal Robbins and his nemesis Warren Harding spearheaded a drive for adventure in the U.S., epitomized by The Nose and Salathé Wall on Yosemite's famous summit El Capitan in the late 1950s. Also in the U.S., John Gill revolutionized bouldering, culminating in 1959 with Red Cross Overhang, which is

Interwar years

Despite the loss of much of a generation, European climbing standards rose quickly, although North America, with its focus on pure exploration, did not catch up until the 1940s. In France, Pierre Allain bouldered the first problem to retain a modern Hueco grade of V2 in 1934. Allain also invented specialized shoes for climbing (thereafter known as PAs). Jack Longland and Chris Preston created some of Britain's first "extreme" climbs (5b/c, or 5.9–5.10), and rising standards began to be consolidated by their compatriots Colin Kirkus, Arthur Birtwhistle and John Menlove Edwards. On the continent Italian climbers, including Emilio Comici, Cesare Maestri and Riccardo Cassin, were celebrities in an era of nationalistic posturing but their achievements were truly world class. Standards developed even faster in Saxony, where Paul Illmer was one of several climbers engaging in face routes equivalent to 5.10 by 1922. The standout ascent of this era, however, was the first ascent in 1938 of the infamous Eiger North Face by the combined German-Austrian team of Anderl Heckmair, Ludwig Vorg, Heinrich Harrer and Fritz Kasparek.

Typical footwear from the postwar years. The PA shoe gradually replaced tennis shoes as the footwear of choice. This photo shows an early mass-produced model made by Ellis Brigham, thereafter known as the EB. The use of nailed boots gradually declined with the invention of vibram soles, as shown here on the Hawkins boot.

now graded at V9. In Britain standards also rocketed, culminating in 1968 with Tom Proctor's Our Father (E4 6b). Bernd Arnold began to dominate climbing in Saxony at a similar level. Mountaineering activities in the Himalayas dominated the media view of climbing throughout this period.

Rock tourists

Englishman Pete Livesey exemplified systematic training in the 1970s, allowing ascents like Right Wall in Snowdonia (E5 6a) and Footless Crow in the English Lake District (E5 6b). Fellow Englishmen John Allen and Steve Bancroft quickly consolidated these grades, but Livesey was one of the first great climbers to travel widely and bring a level of consensus to world standards. Henry Barber continued this trend, representing North America.

The ascent of Everest without oxygen by **Rheinhold Messner and Peter Habeler** captured the public imagination to an unprecedented level and was a significant event in the development of "professional" climbers.

Australian **Rick White** on the infamous bolt ladder near Boot Flake on The Nose of El Capitan (VI, 5.8, A3) in 1973.

Australian climbing quickly developed after the late 1960s, characterized by colorful characters like John Ewbank and Chris Baxter, but it was the international exploits of Kim Carrigan that brought attention to antipodean ability. Other famous travelers included France's Patrick Edlinger and Livesey's ex-protégé Ron Fawcett, who dominated the British scene for nearly a decade.

Millennium end

Fawcett's great rival, John Redhead, helped bring a new level of difficulty gleaned from sport climbing to traditional routes, with bold excursions such as The Bells! The Bells! in North Wales (E7 6b). At Yosemite, Americans Ron Kauk, John Long and John Bachar's 1975 Astroman (5.11c) brought new standards to a long and sustained route. Extensive preparation was now normal for hard new lines, paving the way for technical breakthroughs in the U.S. such as Tony Yaniro's 1979 Grand Illusion at Lake Tahoe (5.13b) and Bill Price's 1980 Cosmic Debris (5.13b) at Yosemite. However, sport climbing grades were bounding ahead, with mid-1980s highlights like Wolfgang Gullich from Germany's Punks in the Gym (31/32) at Arapiles, and Frenchman Anthoine le Menestral's La Rage de Vivre (F8b+) paving the way for early 1990s milestones such as Ben Moon's Hubble (8c+) and Gullich's Action Directe (9a). The era saw a renaissance in "trad" climbing, with standout achievements including John Dunne from the U.K.'s Parthian Shot (E9 7a), American Lynn Hill's free ascent of The Nose of El Capitan at 5.13c and Johnny Dawes from the U.K.'s Indian Face (E9 6c).

The 21st century

While the top standards have only crept up to perhaps 5.15 at the time of writing (for example, Chris Sharma's Realization at Ceuse, France), rapid and on-sight repeats have become commonplace in the 5.14 grades. In

Derek Hersey free-soloing Vertigo Direct (5.12) in Colorado in the early 1980s. Hersey epitomized the free spirit of climbing both in his lifestyle and in his love of solo climbing, which sadly ended with his death in 1993.

Yosemite, big-walls are regularly climbed at racing speed, including several free-ascents by the exceptionally talented German brothers, Alex and Thomas Huber. In Scotland Dave MacLeod's Rhapsody has been given the grade of E11 7a, with reported 50 ft (15 m) falls onto tiny wires. American Ron Kauk has continued to operate for 30 years at the highest levels, producing the Magic Line (5.14a) in 1997, arguably still the world's hardest crack climb.

CLIMBING GREATS

Climbing has produced so many great characters during its history that only some of the most influential figures are described here, all role models in their own ways.

Hermann Buhl

Born in 1924, but tragically killed at the age of 33, Austrian climber Hermann Buhl had at the time of his death already earned a place among the greatest climbers of all time. His strength, endurance and confidence were legendary. Feats including his return bike ride across the Alps to make the first solo ascent of the North Face of Piz Badile have passed into climbing folklore. High points include his solo first ascent of the final obstacles on Nanga Parbat in the Himalayas in 1953. Buhl's first ascent of Broad Peak with fellow Austrian legend Kurt Diemberger in 1957 was another outstanding achievement but it was his last; days later he fell to his death through a snow cornice on the neighboring peak Chogolisa.

Joe Brown

Born in England in 1930, Joe Brown became one of climbing's most influential figures. Still climbing in his 70s, Joe was a member of the legendary Valkyrie climbing club. He started climbing in 1947 in the English Peak District, using nailed boots at first for both roped climbing and bouldering. He created many iconic routes, including the classic Saul's Crack at the Roaches (HVS 5a or 5.8) in the English Peak District and The Boulder (E1 5a) on Clogwyn du'r Arddu, North Wales. In the Alps, his new route on the Blaitière won international acclaim. In 1955 he and George Band made the first ascent of Kangchenjunga in the Nepalese Himalayas. Many more expeditions followed, including Mustagh and Trango Towers.

Royal Robbins reaching down to retrieve an aider. His big-wall routes have inspired several generations of climbers.

Joe Brown's Fissure Brown on the West Face of Aiguille de Blaitière, (Chamonix, France) climbed in 1954, is still regarded as a hard off-width climb (5.11 equivalent) and attained legendary status in its day.

Royal Robbins

One of the all-time greatest U.S. climbers and ambassadors for the sport, Robbins was born in 1935 and learned to climb at Tahquitz in California (including opening, arguably, the first 5.9 in North America), before making a string of groundbreaking ascents in Yosemite that brought him worldwide recognition. He wrote many influential articles about climbing style and was an early proponent of "clean climbing" (using mainly natural features for protection). His instruction books influenced a generation. Robbins' tales are still a popular lecture attraction and, like many climbers of his generation, he continues to enjoy an adventurous lifestyle.

Rheinhold Messner

Born in the South Tyrol region of Italy in 1944, Rheinhold Messner began climbing at 13. He climbed extensively throughout the Alps and the Dolomites, which inspired his defense of "fair means" in his influential paper, "The Murder of the Impossible." Inspired by Hermann Buhl, Messner turned his attention to the Greater Ranges but the descent of Nanga Parbat in 1970 tragically took his brother's life, and seven of Rheinhold's toes, due to frostbite. The tragedy dogged his life, but Messner went on to make the first ascent of Everest in 1978 with Austrian climber Peter Habeler and beat this feat in 1980 by achieving it solo. He also became the first person to climb all 14 "eight-thousanders"—peaks over 26,000 ft (8,000 m).

Greg Child

Australian climber and author Greg Child is hailed by many as the world's finest all-round climber. Born in 1957 in Sydney, he has achieved many first ascents of rock climbs up to grade 5.13 or its equivalent, pioneered A5 big-walls, and achieved mountaineering feats such as Everest, Gasherbrum IV and K2, as well as exceptionally hard rock spires such as Shivling (India), Shipton and

Rheinhold Messner made many audacious free-solo ascents of hard climbs, particularly in the Italian Dolomites, as pictured here in 1979.

Lobsang Spires (Pakistan) and Great Sail Peak (Baffin Island) in a career spanning over 30 years. Child is a prize-winning author and filmmaker, and has lived in the U.S. since 1980 after falling in love with Yosemite. In recent years Child has turned his attention to the exploration of jungles and deserts but still continues to climb at the highest levels.

Wolfgang Gullich

Wolfgang Gullich was born in Ludwigshafen, Germany, in 1960, and was one of the most charismatic rock climbers of all time. He increased standards by several grades over a golden decade that ended with his untimely death in a road accident in 1992. Gullich learned to climb in the Pfalz area, making a free ascent of Jubiläumsriss (VII-) at just 16. From 1984 onward, he grabbed the headlines with routes that culminated in the groundbreaking

Action Directe (XI or 9a) at Frankenjura. Its series of dynamic moves using single-finger pockets led him to invent the campus board.

Catherine Destivelle

Born in Algeria in 1960, but raised in Paris, media darling Catherine Destivelle set the world alight with her exploits for nearly two decades from 1985, when she won a string of international climbing competitions and made early repeats of hard test-pieces such as Chouca (8a+) in Boux, France, before turning her attention to hard climbs in mountain settings. Of these, her solo ascents of both the Bonatti Pillar and a new route on the neighboring West Face are among her most famous climbs, but she has also made some outstanding climbs in the Himalayas, including a free ascent of the Nameless Tower.

Catherine Destivelle has withdrawn from the public gaze but still enjoys climbing at a high standard. Here she tackles a 7a crack on the Grand Capucin, Chamonix, France.

ACCESS AND CONSERVATION

Climbing is an activity that can have minimal impact on the environment, and takes place in areas where nature is rarely in competition with commercial activities. However, there is no automatic right to unrestricted access.

Many crags are situated on land that is under private ownership, where climbers need a good relationship with the owners to ensure continued use. In some cases problems arise due to the landowner's concerns about personal liability for accidents on their land. Some landowners try to charge for access, beyond reasonable maintenance costs. While this may be appropriate for commercial adventure centers it is not acceptable for individual climbers. One of the benefits of providing free access with no permit systems or payment is that the landowner carries minimal liability for crag accidents, an important factor for climbers when negotiating free access.

Some landowners are concerned about a loss of privacy, worrying that hordes of badly behaved tourists will descend upon their land. These preconceptions can be easily reinforced, and climbers should be careful not to antagonize landowners or other users unnecessarily. This will involve parking sensitively, minimizing litter and hygiene problems, refraining from the use of foul language, and avoiding damage to trees, gates and fences.

National parks often have a philosophy that supports and encourages suitable recreational use, and climbing has been accepted by most authorities as fitting within this remit. However, access is limited or even banned in some areas, where recreational activities are believed to be incompatible with the spiritual heritage of the area. Famous examples include Uluru (Ayers Rock) in Australia, and some of Utah's Canyonlands. These areas can be contrasted with places like New Zealand's Whanganui Bay, where an excellent relationship with the local spiritual leader has allowed climbing to be reinstated after temporary difficulties.

Another area of potential conflict is the placement of fixed equipment, and there are areas where fixed gear is banned altogether. Colorful tapes and cords attached to the crag for thread protection points and rappel stations can present unnecessary eyesores. These can be either removed or replaced with camouflaged materials. Bolts are normally less obtrusive but they can shine fiercely in bright sunshine so, where practical, the use of hangers with a matte finish should be encouraged. The clatter made by electric drills when placing bolts can be extremely offensive in a wilderness site, and should only be contemplated after wide consultation with other recreational and conservation bodies with an interest in the area. In any case, drilling should be avoided on busy days and other times when offence is more likely to be caused.

Some popular climbing crags are also the nesting grounds of protected species of birds, or the home of rare plants. Voluntary agreements have often been negotiated with nature conservation bodies regarding access at certain times of year, and these should be adhered to. Guidebooks normally explain the times of operation of any such arrangements, but the situation can change, so always ask local activists and consult current information in climbing publications and on websites to confirm the latest agreements.

Climbers can be proactive in the conservation of the crag environment, starting with simple steps like removing litter and avoiding damage to trees and their roots, perhaps by attaching discreet rappel chains. Before embarking on extensive gardening operations to unearth boulders or crags, climbers should consider the impact on a natural habitat. Sometimes more drastic work such as footpath restoration is needed, but this should always be carried out in consultation with local authorities and landowners.

The cumulative effect of selfishness, laziness and exhaustion can lead to pristine wildernesses becoming spoiled for future generations, and even to a loss of access concessions. Nowhere is this conflict more apparent than on the spiritual pinnacle of mountaineering, Mount Everest. This picture shows **garbage desecrating Everest**, known as Chomolungma (Goddess Mother of the World) in Tibetan. Climbers can work together to turn this tide of human jetsam.

STYLES OF CLIMBING

Unroped climbing

Climbing near the ground without a rope is called bouldering. When climbing on low boulders and walls, the consequences of a slip can be managed either by jumping off or spotting (see *Bouldering* on page 30). This is called free-soloing once the climber is more than a few yards above the ground. Longer solo climbs require a lot of experience and judgment from the climber as there is little room for error. Even deep-water solos (DWSs) require skillful risk analysis as they can result in serious injuries if the landing site has not been carefully inspected.

Climbing with a rope

The use of a rope allows climbers to manage the level of risk for their sport. A climber will normally wear a harness and tie the rope into this, so that the force generated by a fall would be shared between the legs and waist. On steep climbs a harness is vital, as a climber hanging in space from a simple waist tie would quickly suffocate. To protect the climber, another person controls the rope with a friction system: if the climber falls, the rope is locked to stop them from falling too far. This is called belaying. The climb between one belay station (including

Two climbers **slingshot top-roping** on an artificial climbing wall. Note how each rope runs through a large carabiner at the top of the wall and back down to ground level where a belayer handles the rope to provide safety.

the ground) and the next (including the summit) is called a pitch.

Top-roping

This is generally the safest system of roped climbing. An anchor is fastened at the top of the crag and the climber is linked to this with an adjustable length of rope. The belayer at the top of the climb controls this length of rope as the climber ascends, so the rope stays reasonably tight at all times. If the

climber loses contact with the rock for any reason, the result should be a simple slump onto the rope as the belayer locks off the rope. However, few routes take a perfectly straight line, so the fall is likely to include some degree of swinging sideways as well: climbers call this a pendulum. This system can be modified by threading the rope through the top anchor while both the climber and belayer are based at the bottom of the crag. Once

ROPED SOLOING
Some expert climbers occasionally use a compromise system for soloing, involving a rope attached to a belay station and a self-locking device capable of holding a fall. This requires considerable judgment and provides no camaraderie, offering little attraction for climbers.

Climbing a multi-pitch route:
(1) Climber in green leads first pitch.
(2) After seconding first pitch, the climber in purple "leads through" on pitch two. (3) The climber in green completes the climb and can provide a top-rope for his partner.

the climber has reached the top of the climb, they can be lowered back to the ground by the belayer. This system is often called slingshot top-roping. Both systems allow the climber to tackle routes of any level of difficulty without serious consequences if the climbing proves to be too difficult for success.

Lead climbing

Lead climbing requires at least one member of the party to have sufficient experience and confidence in their abilities to begin a climb, trailing rope behind. To safeguard the leader in the event of a fall, the rope is clipped on the way up through a carabiner that is fastened to protection equipment attached to the rock face, to create a threaded anchor called a protection point. This provides a pulley in the event of a fall when the belayer locks the rope using a belay device.

A leader falling from 3 ft (1 m) above a solid protection point will fall until they are 3 ft below the device: at this point

A lead climber clips the rope into a **protection point** on a climbing wall.

the rope begins to absorb energy by stretching and the falling climber soon comes to a halt. In adventure or traditional climbing, the lead climber places the protection equipment where required. In sport climbing the protection points are already in place and are usually provided by bolts that are securely fastened in drilled holes.

At the end of each pitch, the lead climber arranges anchors to create a belay. The second climber can now follow the pitch, effectively top-roping. Climbs vary in length and complexity.

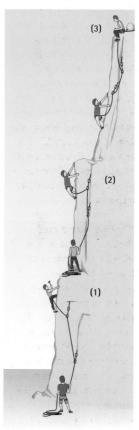

Multi-pitch climbs cannot normally be easily escaped by lowering to the ground. Climbers refer to the difficulty of retreat or serious consequences for error as the level of commitment.

17

INSTRUCTION AND ORGANIZATIONS

Instruction

For safety you should take your first climbing steps with somebody who has at least learned the basic safety procedures. Traditionally, novices learn under the guidance of a mentor, but it is easy to be fooled by impressive tales into assuming that an acquaintance is an expert. Find out just how much climbing your prospective mentor has done, and take things very gradually at first.

A more reliable option is to enlist the services of a qualified instructor. Few countries have a legal requirement for instructors to hold any formal qualifications, and self-qualification is no guarantee of competence. The only internationally recognized professional qualification is membership of the IFMGA (International Federation of Mountain Guides Association). Most countries, however, have some national accreditation scheme involving training and assessment by independent examiners. The AMGA (American Mountain Guide Association) certification is a nationally recognized assessment-based system for qualifying instructors in the United States, but the international club network, Alpine Clubs, also provides instructor training. In the United Kingdom, the national Mountain Training Boards administer basic teaching awards, while MLTUK (Mountain Leader Training UK) administers the professional Mountain Instructor Awards. A comparable structure has been developed in Canada, New Zealand, South Africa and Australia; many other countries also have teaching and coaching awards.

Worldwide standards for training and assessing voluntary rock-climbing instructors are currently accredited by the UIAA

An attentive pair of novices on a **climbing course** learn to handle the ropes.

(Union Internationale des Associations d'Alpinisme), and several countries have attained this accreditation.

Courses

Enrolling in a climbing course is a good way to learn the basics and meet like-minded people. Most climbing gyms run introductory courses, and some also offer courses for outdoor climbing. Residential courses offer more intensive introductory or intermediate development, but a whole week can be very tiring for a novice. Regular short sessions punctuated with recovery days in between are preferable for intermediate to advanced tuition. Courses are advertized in magazines, on the Internet, at climbing gyms, and in brochures for outdoor centers. Make sure you check the qualifications of the instructor to whom you will be assigned.

Organizations

- **Clubs:** Climbing clubs have always been part of the climbing social scene, but some are not for novices and may have strict selection procedures. Offering regular meeting and car-pooling opportunities, some clubs also own accommodation and arrange reciprocal deals with other clubs. Other services include newsletters, equipment discounts and group affiliation to national governing bodies.
- **Governing bodies:** Membership of a national governing body gives democratic power to climbers for both gaining and conserving access to climbs as well as access to grant funding and information databases. Some bodies (e.g., the British Mountaineering Council) also test equipment and produce educational resources, while others (e.g., USA Climbing) only represent sport climbers. At an international level, the UIAA represents climbers' interests, for example, in access and equipment standards.

Sion Idwal Long embarks on his first multi-pitch lead at Sa Gubia, Mallorca. The Mediterranean is a popular destination for **introductory courses**, with excellent sunshine and well-bolted climbs.

GAMES CLIMBERS PLAY

The first rule in climbing is: there are no rules. Climbers are an anarchic breed and shy away from formal definitions of their sport. However, heated debates about what constitutes good style are a common discussion point.

Lito Tejada-Flores defined seven levels of commitment in his seminal article of 1967, "Games Climbers Play." These are: bouldering, crag, continuous, big-wall, alpine, super-alpine and expedition. Each has its own set of style aspirations, that is,

an accepted "perfect" style of ascent, but even this can be improved by transferring the style from a less committing level to one higher up the sequence. The ultimate achievement, therefore, is to attempt a Himalayan peak, solo, with no ropes or technical equipment. It is not always possible to achieve the perfect style, but climbers are expected to describe their style of ascent honestly.

At the heart of the style debate is protection of the climbing environment for

future generations. Thus a balance must be struck between cleaning vegetation from a climb and damaging precious or delicate habitats. In areas where climbing is regarded as an important part of the tourist industry, whole hillsides have been stripped of vegetation to create new crags. By contrast, killing a single plant could have a disastrous impact on access in other areas, so it is vital that any modifications to the crag environment are made after full consultation with the local community.

TAKE NOTE

Any climb that has been completed in less than perfect style is open to improvement from subsequent climbers. However, this does not automatically give the right to remove pitons or bolts if a consensus accepts the "fixed gear."

The idealized style can be defined as combining minimal impact on the environment with no reliance on any aids for progress or resting, other than natural handholds and footholds. Thus the purest style to which all ascents aspire is on-sight free-climbing. This means no prior preparation either by rappel or climbing, and no assistance from artificial aids such as pulling on, or stepping into, slings. Many first ascents accept a compromise from these ideals, often because at the time any other style seemed beyond human capabilities. Inevitably, later ascents have improved on this style through better psychological or physical preparation.

Changing the rock to obtain safety protection probably causes the most controversy, because it robs a more skillful or bolder future generation of the pristine experience they could otherwise have enjoyed. Drilling holes for bolts is regarded as irreversible damage, while hammering pitons into existing cracks also causes damage, especially if repeated regularly. Thus any pitons are generally left in situ, but this then raises issues about corrosion. In many areas regularly spaced bolts and pitons are accepted by consensus within a sport-climbing venue, while in traditional climbing areas, placement of bolts and even pitons are heavily disputed and often rapidly removed.

A climber bouldering in the Indian Himalayas demonstrates the **purest style** that might be transferred to the mountains behind: climbing alone with no ropes or mechanical aids.

GRADES AND GUIDEBOOKS

North America	Australia	United Kingdom Adjectival	United Kingdom Technical	UIAA	France	South Africa	
							EASY
5.1	5	Mod		I	1	6	
5.2	6	Diff			2	7	
5.3	7			II		8	
5.4	8	V Diff		III	2+	9	
5.5	9			III+	3	10	
5.6	10			IV	3+	11	
5.7	11	Severe	4a	IV+	4-	12	
	12			IV+	4	13	
5.8	13		4b	V-		14	
	14	Very Severe		V	4+	15	
	15		4c				
	16	HVS		V+	5a	16	
5.9			5a	VI-	5b		
	17			VI	5c	17	
5.10a	18	E1	5b	6a	18		
				VI+		19	
5.10b	19	E2		VII-	6a+	20	
5.10c	20		5c	6b	21		
5.10d		E3		VII	6b+	22	
5.11a	21		6a	VII+	6c	23	
5.11b	22	E4		VII+	6c+	24	
5.11c	23	E5		VIII-	7a	25	
5.11d	24	E6	6b	VIII	7a+	26	
5.12a	25			VIII+	7b	27	
5.12b/c	26	E7		IX-	7b+/7c	28	
5.12c/d	27		6c	IX	7c+	29	
5.13a	28	E8		IX+	8a	30	
5.13b	29		7a	X-	8a+	31	
5.13c/d	30			X	8b	32	
5.14a	31	E9		X+	8b+	33	
5.14b	32				8c	34	
5.14c	33			XI-	8c+	35	
	34	E10		XI			
5.14d	35		7b		9a	36	
5.15a	36	E11		XI+	9a+	37	
5.15b	37			XII-	9b	38	
5.15c	38			XI	9b+		HARD

Grades

All climbs are graded according to difficulty. Most countries have evolved their own grading systems, inextricably linked with the local rock types, route length and history. However, because all grades start from numerical systems, it is possible to draw up an approximate comparison table.

A technical grade gives an indication of the consensus of opinion on how difficult the climbing moves are. However, most grading systems do not really distinguish between one very hard ("crux") move and a sustained series of slightly easier, but tiring, moves.

The U.K. grading system attempts to overcome this by superimposing an adjectival grade upon the technical standard. The adjectival grade gives an overall impression of the difficulty of an ascent, but the technical grade combines to give more information about the climb. For example, a high technical grade and a low adjectival grade implies a well-protected, short crux (e.g., VS 5a). A low technical grade with a high adjectival grade combination (e.g., HVS 4c) means that the pitch is sustained or serious.

The North American system warns of serious pitches in a more concise way by adding letters such as R (run out) or X (unprotected). As a general rule, this system would move a climb approximately one grade up the British adjectival system for an R rating, and two adjectival grades up for an X rating. The length/commitment of the whole route is also implied using a Grade System of 1 to 5 for free climbs, with Grade 5 routes usually taking more than a day to complete (see *Big-wall Climbing* on page 158).

The French system concentrates on technical difficulty and has therefore been adopted for sport climbing and climbing-gym grading in many areas, including the U.K. The UIAA grading system was an attempt to standardize grades worldwide, but it has not been adopted in

many areas, as home-grown systems are generally preferred.

For bouldering, yet another series of grades is often used, with the most popular systems being the Font(ainebleau) and Hueco (V) grades. Some countries use the same technical grades as for longer climbs, especially for easier problems. Bouldering grades are generally harder than those of longer routes. As an illustration, the relatively low grade of Hueco V5 (the grades extend currently to V15) equates to Font 6c and North American 5.12. However, in reality it would be rare for such a hard crux to be found high up on a 5.12 climb.

Climbing guidebooks

Information about the location of crags and climbs has been published ever since Walter Haskett Smith produced the first rock-climbing guidebook, *Climbing in the British Isles*, in 1894, and "beta" information (to assist an ascent) is also increasingly available on the Internet. Most climbing guides contain information about local facilities such as accommodations and restaurants, as well as important advice about access and accepted style, geology and local climbing history, plus a liberal sprinkling of inspirational photographs.

Guidebooks originally used mainly verbal descriptions of each route, sometimes including detailed moves, but pictorial information has gradually increased. Since the 1980s, a diagrammatic style has developed that uses icon- and symbol-based crag views (superimposed either on a sketch or photograph) called a topo.

> **TIP**
> Topos provide a wealth of information in a very concise form and can also be supplemented where necessary by a short verbal description, so this system is used almost universally for sport climbs and also increasingly for traditional routes.

ROCK TYPES

Rock types

There are so many different types of rocks around the world that a climber will always find new challenges, requiring different skills. Some countries have a huge variety of rock types within a small area, whereas other countries are relatively uniform geologically and their inhabitants might have to travel to extend their repertoire or even find any outcrops at all.

All rocks are basically one of two types: igneous or sedimentary. Various factors can later affect rocks of either type to form a third category—metamorphic. Each rock type has its own characteristics that dramatically affect the texture of the rock and the style of climbing it demands.

Igneous rocks

This type of rock is formed when volcanic activity either squeezes ("intrudes") magma into weaknesses under the Earth's surface (forming plutonic—or underworld—rocks) or forces it to spew out over the land or into the air (volcanic rocks). These dramatic events are followed by various speeds of cooling, which affect the size of the crystals formed and their bonding.

- **Granite** is the best known of the plutonic rocks, varying in color from

Classic **granite climbing** on the East Buttress of El Capitan (5.10b), Yosemite.

white through pink to dark gray. It becomes exposed as softer rocks are eroded from above it. Because it is such a tough rock, it also forms some of the world's largest walls and slabs. Perhaps the most well-known granite features are found in California's Yosemite Valley. Granite climbing is characterized by steep slab climbing (often lacking natural protection).

- **Dolerite** cools from magma that flows through weaknesses and often forms clean-cut hexagonal columns as it cools. Famous examples include the immaculate Devil's Tower in Wyoming and Northern Ireland's Fair Head.

- **Rhyolite** is formed when volcanoes erupt violently at very high temperatures. It is characterized by air pockets, ash deposits and

A typical **sandstone wall** in South Africa's Cape region.

lumps called "bombs." The violence of its formation gives rhyolite great variety and provides some of the very best and most highly featured rocks for climbing.

Sedimentary rocks

As rocks are eroded over the centuries, wind and water (or ice) move the particles and deposit them in layers. Sediment from erosion and dead organisms also collects on sea floors and is later exposed through climate change. Gradually these deposits are crushed under the pressure of layers on top to form various types of rocks.

- **Sandstone** is literally solidified sand, and is among the most abundant rock type. The crystalline grains usually give good friction, and the rock is often fractured, allowing

Left: The author climbing the grit classic Regent Street (E2 5c) in England's Peak District.

Right: Characteristic mountain limestone in the Verdon Gorge of France. The climber is using water-solution pockets (gouttes d'eau) as hand- and footholds.

natural protection placements. Sandstone varies considerably in quality, from the soft, fine-grained texture found in southern England and Germany to the compact sandstone of South Africa's Cape region, Australia's Blue Mountains and desert spires in the U.S. A coarse-grained sandstone known as "grit" is renowned for its climbing quality.

- **Limestone** is made from the calcareous shells of generations of water creatures, originating in beds of evaporated seas and lakes. It is chemically eroded by rainwater and resolidifies where drips emerge from the rock mass. Examples include the characteristic finger pockets of famous crags like Verdon and Orpierre in France, and the flow-and-drip features of the

Greek island Kalymnos, Thailand, Vietnam and Mallorca, Spain.
- **Conglomerates** consist of larger sediments and pebbles naturally cemented together. The pockets and pebbles can give surprising and excellent holds even on overhanging walls, but natural protection is usually unreliable. Examples are Meteora in Greece, and Riglos and Montserrat in Spain.

Metamorphic rocks
Temperature, pressure and/or chemical action can change original rock types. Some are excellent for climbing; others can be very fragile or brittle.
- **Quartzite** is a fused sandstone that often provides fantastic climbing and reasonable natural protection. Famous crags include Australia's Arapiles (Djurid), North Wales' Gogarth and Shawangunks in the eastern U.S.

Jenny Lambert enjoying the excellent quartzite of Arapiles, Australia.

- **Gneiss** is a crushed and often folded rough rock that can form large cliffs of variable quality, like Norway's Troll Wall.
- Of the various rocks metamorphosed from mud, **slate** can provide exciting climbing on tiny edges, often devoid of reliable protection. Even drilled bolts are of dubious value because of the tendency to cleave that makes slate such a good roofing material.

CLIMBING GYMS

Indoor climbing is believed to be one of the fastest-growing sports in the world. Artificial climbing gyms have developed from simple training facilities made largely of brick or wood into sophisticated and popular establishments that have sprung up all around the globe. Most climbing gyms escape the confines of weather with an indoor location, but some use the outside of large structures like dams, bridges or towers. Sometimes the natural stonework can be utilized without modification. Most climbing competitions are held on artificial structures to allow fresh routes to be constructed for each event.

Construction

Climbing gyms originated in the United Kingdom, where the first climbing wall was created in 1964 at Leeds University by Don Robinson, a lecturer in physical education. Consisting of pieces of natural rock inserted into a hallway wall, the Leeds climbing wall was soon imitated by many sports centers. After experiments with many materials, most commercial walls now have an underlying structure of plywood panels with regularly spaced holes, each containing a specially formed T-nut to allow modular handholds and footholds to be bolted to the wall. The modular nature of modern walls allows routes to be regularly changed in order to maintain interest and allow improvements.

The climbing surface is normally rendered with a variety of textured products, including concrete and paint and/or polyurethane loaded with sand. The panels are bolted directly onto walls or skeletal steel structures that allow complex shapes to be constructed, mimicking the architecture of natural crags. Most climbing gyms have areas dedicated to bouldering and a separate area up to

In the **safe environment** of a climbing wall, two climbers practice lead climbing grade 5.10c.

Left: The **climbing gym** is a good place to build a repertoire of technical skills and a hightened sense of balance for harder outdoor routes.

Below: On an **indoor bouldering wall**, graded problems usually use only marked (usually color-coded) holds.

60 ft (20 m) in height for leading with bolt protection, normally with fixed quickdraws plus a double carabiner arrangement at the top to allow both an easy clip for the leader and a locking facility for top-roping. Some smaller facilities only allow bouldering and top-roping.

Shock-absorbent padding lines the floor of a climbing gym, normally with thicker layers under the bouldering sections. It is important that the padded sections butt up tightly together with no gaps.

Many climbers build their own climbing gyms, often known as "woodies" or "cellars." Most use a panel structure but leave the plywood exposed, and are generally used for bouldering only.

Routes and grading

Holds come in various colors, so those of the same color are often used to denote a route, allowing routes of different difficulty levels to be overlaid on top of one another. Sometimes colored tape placed under climbing holds is used to mark different routes. The route is graded on the understanding that a climber is only allowed to use holds of the designated color as handholds, but may be allowed to use surface structures and textures ("features") as footholds: the climbing gym's grading list will specify the rules used.

TAKE NOTE

Commercial climbing gyms require some sort of statement of competence from participants, normally linked to a membership system. Induction training is usually offered for novices before they are allowed to use the facilities independently. Climbing gyms are very sociable places with plenty of distractions, so a systematic approach to safety is essential, particularly when attaching to the rope and preparing to lower off from the top. Avoid standing underneath boulderers, and be ready to both receive and give advice if important safety principles are neglected.

SPORT CLIMBING

In areas where anchors are permanently attached to the rock, climbers can concentrate on the technical difficulties of the climb, without having to search for protection placements while hanging onto tiny holds. This is the principle behind sport climbing, a style that has spread throughout the world since its conception in France during the 1970s.

Sport climbing allows climbers to move unhampered by masses of heavy protection equipment and to concentrate their attention on the technicalities of movement. Traveling with just a bundle of quickdraws and a rope, climbers can fly cheaply to exotic locations, leading to a boom in climbing tourism in recent years.

A sport climber threading the rope through **top anchors** in order to be lowered back to the ground.

Sport vs. traditional climbing

Originally a method of establishing lead climbing in limestone regions with limited opportunities for the natural protection methods used in traditional climbing, sport climbing is generally felt to damage opportunities for adventure when the style encroaches into areas previously reserved for these natural protection placements. This has provoked angry and well-documented controversies, often resulting in the destruction of offending bolt placements. Unfortunately this is always at the expense of the crag environment; thankfully these issues now tend to be discussed at length by local activists before choosing suitable venues for sport climbs.

In many national parks, fixed equipment is regarded as an eyesore and is banned by the local authorities, sometimes leading to a complete moratorium on climbing. By contrast, bolted lowering stations have sometimes been a necessary condition for gaining access in areas where loose bands of rock would otherwise prevent safe exits. Some areas have adventure climbs that are bolt-protected. These bolts are well spaced and usually placed by the lead climber on the way up, often while balanced precariously. Bolts on these climbs are rarely as strong or as secure as those placed on rappel.

ETHICS AND STYLE

Climbers are expected to report the style used for their ascent. The successful "free" ascent involves no hanging on to equipment for resting or progress, but might be preceded by various levels of preparation.

- **On-sight flash:** Climbed from the ground in one go, placing quickdraws, first attempt, no prior in-depth knowledge or inspection
- **On-sight beta flash:** As above, but with prior information (beyond guidebook description)
- **Red point:** A clean ascent, but made after prior preparation
- **Pink point:** As above, but with quickdraws preplaced on bolts
- **Dogging (hangdogging):** Hanging on to equipment in between attempts to work out a move

Fixed equipment

Sport climbs are characterized by drilled equipment placements. These may be supplemented with pitons hammered into cracks and by webbing attached to natural threads.

Bolt hangers are fixed using either epoxy-resin glue or by tightening an expansion bolt. Placing bolts requires skill, and a degree of maintenance is required. Initially, the resin must bond properly and expansion bolts be correctly tightened. Subsequently, the stability of the surrounding rock should be examined and the bolt itself observed for signs of corrosion or movement. Climbers should never accept the safety of an individual bolt hanger without question.

Length

Many sport pitches are designed to be climbed using a single rope, so the maximum pitch length is less than half a rope length, allowing the climber to be lowered back to the ground. However, average rope lengths have gradually increased to accommodate longer pitches, and consequently 130 ft (40 m) pitches are not uncommon. Multi-pitch climbs have also been equipped as sport climbs, and these usually have longer pitches requiring double ropes for rappel descents. Some routes are too steep for normal retreats by rappel.

Adventure

Die-hard traditionalists argue that sport climbing removes the element of adventure from climbing, and watching climbers hanging from bolts to practice moves could lead some to the same conclusion. However, the possibility of a painful fall exists, and many bolted climbs have spaced protection, or wild, committing locations where a sense of adventure is guaranteed.

A sport climber **clipping a quickdraw** into a bolt. Clipping the rope into the bottom carabiner requires practice.

BOULDERING

In many ways bouldering is both the simplest and purest form of climbing. No ropes or harnesses are used, and the only requirement is a piece of rock or, failing that, the outside or inside of a building. Bouldering has been practiced since the 19th century but has seen a massive surge in popularity over the last decade, leading to an explosion in standards as well as a complete fashion industry in clothing and equipment.

Although bouldering can be practiced alone, it is usually a very sociable activity, with climbers taking turns to attempt a problem and to provide protection in the event of an awkward fall. Some problems may require hundreds of attempts before success is achieved.

Falling

This is an inevitable aspect of bouldering, especially when attempting difficult problems, and care must be taken to minimize injuries. Check the landing site for rocks and other obstructions and remove any that are portable. If a move proves to be too hard, reverse or jump before losing control. For taller boulders with a long fall

potential it is sensible to check the finishing moves and descend if possible before getting committed a long way above the ground. Sometimes the only way to do this is by practicing on a top-rope.

At the end of a long day spent on multi-pitch routes, **bouldering** is a great way to practice some difficult moves just a few feet above ground.

An **attentive spotter** safeguarding a boulderer attempting to climb an overhang.

Crash mats

These are vital for cushioning awkward landings. Gone are the days when climbers might use an old mattress; nowadays purpose-built crash mats are de rigueur. Modern mats are easily portable and provide excellent

A typical **bouldering mat** folds in half for carrying.

energy absorption, normally by combining a hingeing or wrapping system with layers of different density foam lining. Carrying straps allow the mat to be moved while keeping the hands free.

Spotting

Teamwork can dramatically reduce the likelihood of injuries if a boulderer falls awkwardly. Spotting involves fellow climbers standing below or behind the climber in readiness to field a fall by catching the faller's shoulders and guiding the feet to a safe landing spot, away from any obstacles. On steep problems the spotter will support the climber under the shoulders so that the feet can swing down first. Successful spotting requires total concentration, because the boulderer might only commit to the move on the basis that a fall will be successfully fielded. The spotter's hands may hover inches away from the climber's back but should not offer any physical contact unless stopping a fall.

Free-soloing

Longer boulder problems blur with free-soloing, as there comes a point when to fall is unthinkable. Free-soloing involves total commitment and can bring a huge sense of achievement, but it carries the highest penalty—the price of an error can be a serious injury or even death. Free-soloing should never be undertaken by inexperienced climbers, as it requires very fine judgment

about conditions and personal form. For every successful world-class exponent such as John Bachar there are several who have died, so never let peer pressure influence your decision to attempt a free-solo climb.

Deep-water soloing

Climbs above deep water allow a thrilling but safer variation of unroped climbing, as a fall is less likely to cause serious injury. Even so, it is important to check the landing, as different tide levels can expose or hide rocks below the surface. Deep-water soloing can be a very rewarding and sociable activity, and occasionally large gatherings are organized, attracting hundreds of participants. Some exceptionally hard climbs have been completed as deep-water solos, sometimes finishing dangerously high above the water.

Adrenaline-packed **deep-water soloing**, high above the sea. For experienced climbers only.

ADVENTURE CLIMBING

Traditional (or trad) climbing is at the heart of all adventure climbing; indeed, the two terms are almost synonymous. Whether on a single pitch or a multi-day epic, the basic premise is the same. The lead climber embarks on a pitch, placing protection equipment either in cracks or draped over or around features. When protection features run out, the leader has to commit boldly to attempting the moves unprotected with the potential for an ever-increasing fall: it is all about calculated risk.

Some adventure climbs accept the compromise of bolt protection at belay stations but, with a few notable exceptions, bolts are not acceptable as protection on the pitch. Similarly, the preplacement of protection equipment is not regarded as fulfilling the spirit of adventure climbing. At the time of writing, a few infamous bold climbs—e.g., The Lion (5.12b, X), Boulder, U.S.—still await a genuine adventure lead, and are still regarded as the epitome of climbing style.

Single-pitch climbs
Cliffs that are less than a rope length in height are

A climber jams a steep crack with **hand-placed protection**. A strong climber can hang on to place plenty of protection here.

ETHICS AND STYLE
An on-sight free ascent (or "flash") is the ideal style, but various types of preparation are often made and declared by the climber.
- **Rappel inspection:** The holds are examined and perhaps brushed from the safety of a rappel rope
- **Top-rope inspection:** The climb is first top-roped to check the moves are possible for the leader
- **Yo-yo:** A kind of war of attrition, placing pieces of protection on the lead but lowering to a rest between attempts, allowing the moves below to be efficiently top-roped on the way back to the high point
- **Head point:** A clean lead of a poorly protected climb after extensive top-rope practice, it often utilizes protection preplaced by rappel.

often climbed in a single pitch. Despite the relatively short length, these climbs can feel psychologically committing to lead due to the potential for long falls. A climber can normally retreat, though, and rescue from above is an option. It is often possible to walk around to the top and fasten anchors to allow the practice of top-roping, dropping a rope down the crag and protecting the climber from above. This is a useful form of training but is not regarded as adventure climbing.

Top left: A climber is days away from help on **Great Trango Tower** in Pakistan's Karakorum.

Above: Not all climbs end with a summit like this one on the **Eichorn's Pinnacle**, Tuolumne (U.S.). The level of commitment is clearly visible here, where the descent will involve rope-work.

Multi-pitch climbs

These climbs are split by intermediate belay stations, and may vary in length up to many dozens of pitches. Speed is of the essence on longer routes, and it may become necessary to pull up on protection equipment in order to escape the route before nightfall. Enforced nights out, or bivouacs, are not unknown on these climbs, as it can be difficult to retreat from above a certain belay: the "point of no return."

Sea cliff climbs

The crashing of waves, rappel approaches and tidal encroachment can combine to make sea cliffs feel overwhelmingly adventurous. For some climbs, once established, the only practical escape is by completing the ascent. Many sea cliffs are only visible by air or boat, so the chances of rescue may be very slim.

WHAT TO WEAR

Clothing

There are no special clothing requirements for climbing. The practical requirements are protection from the elements and against abrasion, plus freedom of movement. For warmer climates, cargo shorts or capris are an excellent choice, combined perhaps with a T-shirt for sun protection. A windproof jacket is a sensible addition for multi-pitch climbs, and can be tied around the waist when it is not needed. For cooler conditions, extra clothing is useful for the belayer, including some light leather gloves, which also give protection for rope handling. Climbers are often led by fashion, and some significant first ascents have been achieved in quite impractical clothing in the pursuit of sartorial elegance.

Helmets

A climbing helmet is a sensible acquisition. It will give you a degree of protection from falling rocks and absorb some of the impact in a head-first fall, plus provide varying degrees of protection in the event of a pendulum.

Only a helmet tested with the specific requirements of climbing should be used, but a rather bewildering choice is available. Until fairly recently, helmets were mostly made of fiberglass, and were invariably heavy and uncomfortable. Ultra-lightweight "lids" are also now available, but there is always a degree of tradeoff between protection and weight. Different materials absorb impact in different ways and, on the whole, heavier helmets provide better protection against rock fall and head-first falls, while the light plastic/foam helmets (rather similar in appearance to cycling helmets) can offer better protection against pendulum swings.

Fiberglass helmets need careful handling to prevent chipping and cracking, but they are not prone to the brittle hardening that forces plastic helmets to be retired after only a few years. Try on a variety of helmets and choose one that sits well on your head without sliding backward or forward and thus exposing important parts of the skull. A degree of easy adjustment for both head diameter and chin position will allow you to cater to a wider variety of temperatures by wearing a hat underneath.

Being able to move freely as well as having pockets for essentials are the main priorities when choosing climbing wear. **Lightweight clothing** can be supplemented by layers and long sleeves for colder conditions.

You will notice that many climbers choose not to wear head protection on more solid crags (especially climbing gyms). However, the ability to make an objective risk assessment calls for plenty of experience. All too often the decision is made on fashionable grounds instead, but be warned: there is nothing cool about a skull fracture.

Helmets should be retired if subjected to heavy impact, even if dropped heavily, as the helmet will become deformed when absorbing impact. Fiberglass tends to show damage readily with cracks and chips in the resin. Damage to plastic is harder to spot, so keep track of the helmet's usage. Cracks may form on the shell, and some helmets have a chessboard pattern of ribs inside the dome, designed to show signs of stress by cracking. Also check for damage to the cradle and its attachment points.

WHAT TO TAKE WITH YOU

The amount of equipment carried on a climb varies according to the level of commitment involved. Roadside crags and boulders can be reached with equipment stashed simply in plastic bags, and for sport climbing, a rope bag with free space for a harness and quickdraws may prove adequate; but for most situations a backpack with at least a 2,100 cu-in (30 L) capacity is better, with 2,750 cu-in (45 L) backpacks being the best choice for mountain routes. For multi-pitch routes and sea cliffs, consider taking a small backpack or fanny pack for the second climber to wear. This could contain a shared water supply—a couple of pints (just over a liter) is normally adequate; high-energy snacks; SPF cream; some rappel webbing, or spare prusik cord; the guidebook/route description; a spare fleece; a lightweight head lamp; lightweight sneakers/sandals if the descent is by foot.

In any case, a basic first-aid kit in a watertight container is a sensible idea. The amount of emergency equipment you take needs to be weighed against the level of risk involved—it's easy to escape from a roadside boulder, for example—and the practicalities of carrying extra equipment that will only be used in an emergency. A few small items can be kept in a plastic bag and slipped into a shirt pocket, perhaps including latex gloves, a small penknife, a roll of finger-tape, a triangular bandage and a wound dressing or a sanitary towel.

On routes where retreat or escape would be more complex than just a few rappels, it may be advisable for both climbers to carry backpacks, containing a waterproof jacket each, extra snacks, a second head lamp, and a two-person group shelter (e.g., a shaped nylon sheet), as well as the items listed above.

An **emergency kit** consisting of a fanny pack, light waterproof jacket, serrated knife, mini head lamp, mini first-aid kit and prusik loops.

FOOTWEAR

Climbers use foot-hugging shoes with a rubber strip extending over the toe, sides and heel to maximize adhesion to the rock. Good footwork is absolutely fundamental to climbing. Poor shoes will hinder your development, as the assumption that feet slide off of small holds will take years to overcome if early climbs are undertaken in sloppy rock shoes. All modern shoes use high-grade "sticky" rubber, a development that revolutionized climbing in the early 1980s.

Don't use "hand me downs" unless they fit well and have intact rubber soles. To buy a pair of rock shoes, you will need to visit a specialized climbing store with a reasonable selection of equipment. Try out a variety of shoes, because they come in a bewildering number of shapes and sizes. Some are better suited to wide feet, some are narrow fitting, and the more expensive shoes are built around an asymmetric last for each foot.

Get a comfortable pair. Modern shoes do not stretch much as they age, but feet swell with heat, so shoes that feel tight in the store will be painful on the crag. For climbing gyms and sport routes you can get away with tighter shoes as they will be in use for only minutes at a time, but for progressing to multi-pitch climbing, choose shoes that can be worn all day with comfort. You will notice that most climbers put shoes over bare feet to increase sensitivity. However, a pair of shoes bought to fit over a thin pair of socks allows greater warmth and are more hygienic.

An incredible variety of climbing shoes is available. The choice between rock boot, shoe and slipper is up to you. It is also possible to climb in quality mountaineering boots, but these are only really suitable for routes with square-cut holds, because stiff boots demand an "edging" style of footwork. (See *Using the Feet Effectively* on page 92.)

- **Rock boots** cover the ankle to give increased protection and support on crack climbs and long routes, plus descents down scree or gullies, but limit ankle flexibility—you will be able to reach about 2 in (5 cm) further in shoes by lifting your heels high and standing on tiptoe.
- **Climbing shoes** allow freedom of movement while giving good support on small edges and precision for heel hooking.
- The ultimate for feel and flexibility are **rock slippers**—they are also cheaper and have the advantage of being easily slipped off the heel for comfort while belaying. These are less suitable for your first pair of climbing shoes, however, as the increased sensitivity is at the expense of edging and heel support, which are more important in the early stages of your climbing career.

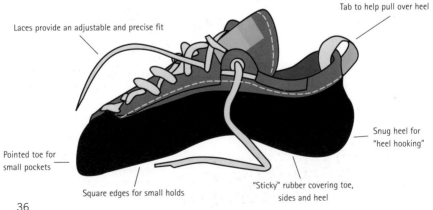

Laces provide an adjustable and precise fit

Tab to help pull over heel

Pointed toe for small pockets

Square edges for small holds

Snug heel for "heel hooking"

"Sticky" rubber covering toe, sides and heel

TIP

The life of rock shoes can be extended by having them resoled when the rubber wears out. This can rejuvenate a favorite comfortable pair, but their performance will inevitably be altered slightly.

A rock-climbing boot gives excellent ankle protection. Ideal for long climbs in rough terrain.

A rock-climbing shoe with laces gives a precise fit and excellent ankle flexibility.

TIP

Climbing in mountaineering boots from time to time is an interesting exercise for developing your footwork.

A Velcro climbing shoe (VCS) is very easy to adjust and remove, but beware of Velcro popping open on small holds.

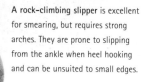

A rock-climbing slipper is excellent for smearing, but requires strong arches. They are prone to slipping from the ankle when heel hooking and can be unsuited to small edges.

37

HARNESSES

A harness is an essential attachment point between the climber and the rope. Originally this was just a waist belt, often referred to as a "swami." Light and simple, the swami does, however, have a major drawback: it gives no leg support and a climber trapped hanging in midair would quickly suffocate. The "sit harness," developed from the original prototype designed by British mountaineer Don Whillans, and improved by the American Forrest design, has now become the standard harness type for rock-climbing activities.

Gear
loop

Leg loop buckle

A simple, fully **adjustable** **harness**. The attachment point is too high for advanced climbers, though.

Choosing a harness

A properly fitted harness should feel comfortable, and spread the load between the climber's thighs and waist. Some harnesses are designed for a longer pelvis, with women in mind. The harness you choose should allow the waist belt to fit snugly around the waist—not the hips—when the leg loops are fastened comfortably around the upper thigh.

Choose a harness with a central attachment point, usually referred to as a belay loop. This is actually the strongest

part of most harness designs and is very convenient for attaching a sling or carabiner with belay/rappel device. For descents this is an important consideration.

Some harnesses are designed to facilitate unfastening the leg loops while still retaining the waist tie, in order to allow climbers to attend to calls of nature. For male climbers this is only an advantage for longer climbs, but women may prefer such a design. Most harnesses also have thin loops of cord or plastic for carrying equipment—these must never be used as belay attachment points. Gear loops are invaluable for storing protection equipment, but check that the loops extend sufficiently toward the front of the harness—some harnesses have gear loops set further back to leave room for the buckle, and these can be awkward to clip. It is a good idea to store the belay device toward the back of the harness to avoid the mistake of leaving it clipped to the gear loop for belaying or rappelling.

A lightweight **performance harness**, with simple waist adjustment and comfortable padding but minimum fittings.

TIP

If you need to use the same harness in a variety of temperatures, get adjustable leg loops that you can alter when wearing extra layers.

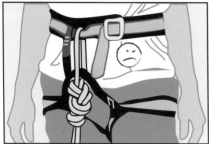

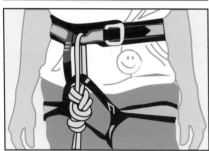

When **locking buckles**, look at the metal plate. An "O" shape (left) means open. A "C" shape (below left) means closed. Make sure it is closed.

> **TIP**
>
> Climbing companions should get in the habit of checking each other's harness fastenings before embarking on a climb.

Fastening a harness

To be safely fastened, a harness buckle must be closed in accordance with the method advised by the manufacturer's instructions. Some harnesses have simple buckles that are slid open and shut, so they never come fully undone. These buckles just need to be pulled reasonably tight. Many designs, however, require the webbing to be doubled back in order to be safely locked. For any buckle there should be at least 4 in (10 cm) of tail once the buckle is attached.

Children and large adults should wear full-body harnesses, as these have a higher attachment point and cannot slide off of the hips if inverted.

Always buy a harness from a reputable dealer, as using a second-hand harness is potentially dangerous unless you have a good knowledge of its previous use, and are confident the recommended life expectancy has not been exceeded. Any harness should be inspected regularly for signs of wear or damage and should be destroyed if there is any doubt. The life expectancy is a maximum of about 10 years, according to most manufacturers.

A fully adjustable harness with plenty of gear loops and buckles on the leg straps. The rear buckles allow the leg loops to be unclipped for calls of nature.

CLIMBING ROPES

Construction

Modern ropes use a kernmantle (sheath and core) type of construction, where the inner core contains braided load-bearing fibers running the whole length of the rope with no joins. The sheath is largely for protection of the inner core, but it does contribute significantly (10–25 percent) to the strength of the rope.

Dynamic climbing ropes can stretch to absorb energy when a leader falls. This elasticity plays a vital role in reducing the forces exerted on the climber's body and the anchors, known collectively as the "safety chain." For nonleading situations such as rappelling, prusiking or top-roping, a low-stretch "semi-static" rope may be more appropriate as the rope will not be needed to absorb as much energy.

Rope sizes

Dynamic rope specifications describe the configuration with which the rope is designed to be used. Single ropes can be used alone and are tested as a single rope with multiple leader falls. These ropes are popular for sport climbing and also for either single-pitch climbs or longer routes with pitches that do not zigzag too much. Single ropes average between 9.5 mm and 11 mm in diameter. For longer routes, a second rope for use on rappels is often used—it is often much thinner (6–8 mm). These second lines are referred to as haul lines or tag lines. Twin ropes are intended for both ropes to be clipped into every protection point when leading, but allow full pitch-length rappels when connected together for descent. These ropes can be very thin—usually somewhere around 8 mm in diameter. Due to the high impact force and high elasticity, twin-rope systems are rare outside the European Alpine regions. The ropes of choice for complex traditional climbs are double (or "half") ropes. These can be clipped into alternating anchors and are strong enough individually to hold leader falls, although a long leader fall from above a belay to below it would severely test this type of rope (see *Constructing Safe Belays* on page 58). Half ropes average about 9 mm in diameter.

Care and storage

Climbing ropes should be protected from corrosive chemicals and should be washed

> **TIP**
>
> A badly damaged rope is best cut through completely to prevent accidental use in the future.

after contact with sea water or after use in gritty or muddy conditions; this prevents salt crystals from causing internal damage or dirt from spoiling the rope's handling qualities. Dry the rope thoroughly, then store it away from direct sunlight, heat sources or potential contaminants.

When handling a rope, check its feel and appearance for any signs of damage such as distorted sections or a visible core. Downgrade the rope to top-rope or rappel if it is subjected to big impact falls or shows signs of any minor damage. Significant furring of the sheath is an indication that many outer fibers have been damaged, whereas a smooth, "glassy" scar running along a section of the rope is a clear sign of friction damage. Ropes marked in this way are suspect—there is no way of telling what has happened to the core.

Lifespan
This depends on how much the rope is used. With frequent but careful outdoor use, a climbing rope should last at

least a year. With infrequent or indoor use, a rope may last much longer—follow the manufacturer's guidelines.

Slings/runners (webbing)
Normally factory-sewn in various lengths, slings are made either entirely from nylon or mixed with white strands of exceptionally strong polyethylene to produce Dyneema or Spectra slings. The two main lengths for slings are 24 in (60 cm) or 48 in (120 cm), which can be conveniently carried over one shoulder. The greater strength of Dyneema allows thinner and lighter slings, but these are more prone to heat damage and the ends should be stitched together rather than knotted.

There are several ways to **coil a rope**. This approach allows the rope to be carried over one shoulder. (1) Tuck one end back on itself to make a loop. (2) Wrap the other end tightly around. (3) Finished rope coil with optional final locking knot.

PROTECTION EQUIPMENT

Development

Early climbers used nothing other than the rope to protect their climbs, so their adage was: "the leader never falls." As safety standards rose, climbers began to carry lengths of cord to loop over spikes and tie around threads. Steel carabiners became widely available as ex-military equipment after World War II, allowing the rope to be clipped into a piece of protection rather than having to untie from the rope in order to thread the piece.

Opportunities for protection were further developed by gathering pebbles, which then had rope wound around them and were inserted into cracks as stoppers that could be threaded. In the 1950s, machine nuts were adapted to create prethreaded artificial "stoppers." Alloy versions followed, and by the 1970s a wide range of protection placement equipment was commercially available. The most recent real innovation was the invention of spring-loaded camming devices in the late 1970s, which allowed rapid deployment in a wide range of crack sizes. The modern rack is lighter and more color-coordinated than its counterpart 20 years ago, but little else has changed.

Carabiners (biners) and quickdraws

Both locking and nonlocking carabiners are essential components of any climbing rack. Providing the link between the various elements in the safety chain, they need to be strong and hard-wearing. A quickdraw is a short sling with a carabiner at each end. One carabiner is used to clip into a piece of protection—the climbing rope is clipped into the other. Wire gates have recently become

Four types of carabiner:
(1) Standard D-shaped snaplink
(2) Wiregate (3) Standard D-shaped locking (4) HMS (pear-shaped) locking

popular, representing a significant weight reduction. Locking carabiners are used when maintaining connection is vital, notably for attaching the rope to a belaying system. Some have a self-locking design usually called a twist-lock, while others—known as HMS or pear-shaped—are designed for use with a friction hitch or multiple knots and have one wide end.

> **TAKE NOTE**
>
> Carabiners are designed to be loaded along the back edge. The nonlocking type are light and convenient for general use. They should have a minimum rating of 4,540 lb (20 kN) with the gate closed and at least about 1,600–1,800 lb (7–8 kN) even with the gate open.

Wired nuts

A range of shaped metal wedges with a threaded wire loop are available. The main set includes wires from about 1/5 in (5 mm) through to 1 1/4 in (30 mm) wide, but micro wires are available for cracks as small as about 1/25 in (1 mm). The larger sizes are also available on rope loops, which are less likely to be rotated out by rope movements.

Hexcentrics

These offset hexagonal nuts can be used as a simple wedge but the offset shape also allows them to cam tighter if placed so that pulling the rope cord forces a rotational movement. Like all nuts, they can be placed sideways to fit cracks when a larger size is not available.

Active (spring-loaded) camming devices

Variously known as ACDs, SLCDs or often by the original trade name, Friends, these are all spring-loaded, so the three or four cams are pushed into contact with the rock. Pulling the stem exerts greater pressure, holding the device in place. These are very effective when well placed but require skill both to deploy and remove. Cams are available to fit in cracks from less than 2/5 in (1 cm) to over 12 in (30 cm) in width.

A TYPICAL BEGINNER'S RACK

- 8 quickdraws of varying lengths
- 2 long slings, or 1 long sling and a cordelette
- 3 short slings
- 10 wired nuts (numbers 1 through 10)
- 3 hexes on cord (numbers 7, 8, 9)
- 10 nonlocking carabiners
- 1 HMS locking biner
- 2 D-shaped locking biners
- 1 nut-extracting tool
- 1 belay device

LATER ADDITIONS

- 3 camming devices (SLCDs) (numbers 1, 2, 3)
- A few micro nuts
- Second set of wired nuts

A typical **intermediate rack** with a selection of nut sizes, slings and cams, quickdraws, a couple of locking carabiners and a nut-extracting tool.

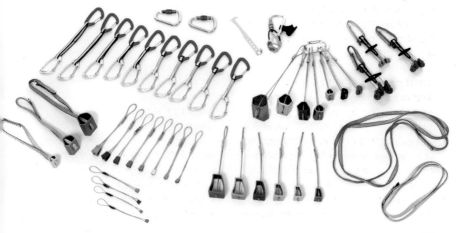

BELAYING AND RAPPELLING DEVICES

All belay devices work on the same basic principle: by forcing the rope into a tight "Z" shape, opposing forces are created that allow an outward pull to be easily held using the resulting friction. By understanding how different sorts of belay devices operate, you can handle ropes more safely than by accepting your friends' or mentors' methods at face value.

Belay devices inevitably compromise between ease of paying out rope and holding power in the event of a fall. Fast devices are categorized as "slick," while holding devices are called "grabbing." For most climbers, a device somewhere in the middle of this spectrum is a sensible choice.

Belay plates

These are all basically variations of the original Sticht plate—one or two holes in a bar or tube through which a loop (or two loops) of rope is passed and clipped into a carabiner to create friction while allowing movement when required.

The small surface area of belay plates means they are less able to dissipate heat than other rappelling devices. By the end of a long rappel the plate may become quite hot, and it

Belay devices:
(1) Single-rope controller, virtually self-locking.
(2) Wedge-shaped plate allows variable friction by rotation, i.e., choosing whether to run the rope around the thick or thin end of the wedge.
(3) ATC "slick" belay device.

A belay device in **locking mode** for safeguarding a difficult move.

Some **locking carabiners** have a device to check the gate is shut and keep the weight loading along the back bar. This plastic component hinges over the gate when it is properly locked.

is all too easy to drop the device; the ribbed texture of some devices (e.g., the Tuber) are an attempt to reduce this problem.

It is advisable to inspect belay plates for wear fairly regularly, especially if the same device is used for rappelling.

Figure-eight devices

Designed primarily for rappelling, these devices create friction by configuring the rope into a "Z" shape, weaving around either the large hole for normal use, or around the small hole when greater friction is required. With the increased use of single ropes on bolt-protected routes, these devices have seen something of a renaissance in recent years. However, for climbers who use double ropes,

even a large figure-eight device is awkward to use, and has the potential for allowing the ropes to melt in the event of slippage.

The grigri

This device is a relative newcomer to the field, working on a similar principle to car seatbelts, where a shock loading will tighten a sprung camming system and hold the rope. Unlike other belay devices, the grigri functions automatically. However, this can work against the instinctive reaction of anybody who has used other belay devices, leading to potential problems with transference of skills. The grigri does not allow dynamic belaying (i.e., progressively slowing the rope movement), so a large impact force results.

The grigri has a diagram of the threading arrangement for the rope engraved on the plate—a useful reminder. It also comes with extensive instructions about safe use of the device.

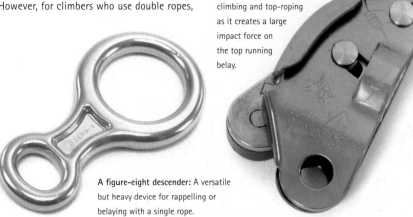

A grigri: Best used for sport climbing and top-roping as it creates a large impact force on the top running belay.

A figure-eight descender: A versatile but heavy device for rappelling or belaying with a single rope.

FIXED EQUIPMENT

Pitons

Pitons (or "pegs") consist of an eye for attaching a carabiner or sling, and a shaft to be inserted into a crack. They range in size from tiny postage-stamp-sized blades called RURPs (Realized Ultimate Reality Pitons) through to huge metal wedges up to 8 in (20 cm) wide called bongs. The larger sizes have been mainly superseded by nuts and camming devices but may still be encountered in situ on routes. Pitons are not normally removed once firmly placed, as repeated removal damages the rock.

Pitons are normally tapped into place using a piton hammer. The correct size piton should push in by hand about halfway in—the remaining shaft is then driven in. An ideal placement should have the eye flush with the rock surface to minimize leverage. Poor placements project further from the crack and it is difficult to assess how much security they offer.

Most pitons are made from hardened steel and therefore are prone to corrosion, especially if placed in sea cliffs, so they should not be trusted without conducting some simple tests. If the eye of the peg and the metal in contact with the rock show significant flaking or distortion, this is a clear sign of damage. The best test for any piton is to clip a quickdraw and watch the peg carefully as the quickdraw is jerked downward. Rotation of the blade or severe flexing demonstrates that the piton is not to be trusted.

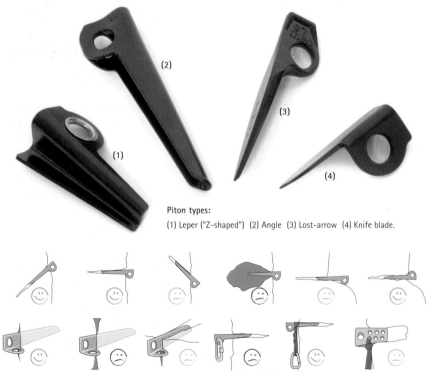

Piton types:
(1) Leper ("Z-shaped") (2) Angle (3) Lost-arrow (4) Knife blade.

A selection of **piton placements**. The good ones use mechanical torquing and minimize leverage. The piton shown at bottom right is a bong.

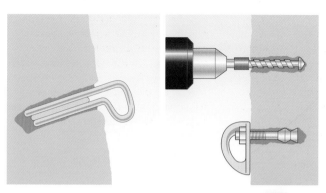

Left: **A glue-in bolt** requires a single large hole, while some "staples" require two narrower holes. Cleaning the hole and twisting the metal into the glue is important for proper bonding. Right: **Expansion bolts** are easier to place but are more prone to corrosion damage and gradually working loose.

Bolts

Bolts are normally found on sport climbs, but some adventure routes have bolt belay stations. In some areas bolted protection can even be found on a pitch classed as adventure climbing, but only in the absence of alternative protection where a slip would otherwise have disastrous consequences.

Glue-in bolts normally have the shape of a rounded staple and may be inserted into one or possibly two smaller holes. Expansion bolts normally consist of an alloy hanger attached by a nut. The nut should be reasonably tight, although rotation of the hanger is not a problem. In some areas, notably in Australia, a "carrot" arrangement is used, where only a protruding nut head is left in the rock and lead climbers carry hangers or wires that are looped over the head; these are then removed by the second climber. This retains more of a sense of adventure, as the bolt is both difficult to see and to clip.

Bolts are checked in the same way as pitons. These can and should be tested for downward and outward pulls, and also checked for rotation. Bolts that can be moved should be treated with great caution.

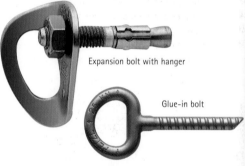

Expansion bolt with hanger

Glue-in bolt

Threads

Some climbs have cord or webbing threads already in place—increasingly, a material with a similar color to the surrounding rock is used, to minimize visibility. These should be carefully examined for signs of wear such as discoloration or significant furring or cuts. The rock or tree should also be examined for signs of weakness or damage, as even the strongest cord is only as good as the anchor to which it is attached (see also page 80).

Jammed nuts and cams

These are usually left in place due to problems experienced by a previous team. As a general rule they should be removed, as they detract from the climbing experience for other parties and gradually corrode over time. Occasionally a very difficult placement is left in position after the first ascent and will be mentioned in the guide description; however, these also corrode over time. Some routes contain decrepit wires or cams blocking the only suitable protection placement and have become dangerous as a result.

ADVANCED AND SPECIALIZED EQUIPMENT

Ascenders

Some climbing activities demand an ability to ascend or pull heavy loads using the rope—in particular, rescues, big-wall climbs and roped access. For these situations mechanical ascenders are much easier to use than prusik cord.

Standard ascenders are still often referred to by their original trade name: jumars. These are too bulky and heavy to carry for most typical climbing situations, but are extremely effective for climbing ropes and also for hauling. A spring-loaded spiked wheel squeezes the rope inside a collar, allowing the device to travel in one direction only, and most standard ascenders also incorporate a comfortable handle. Climbing a rope using a pair of these devices is often called "jugging."

This typical **ascender** is designed for left-handed use.

A small lightweight device can easily be carried on a climber's harness, perhaps with a couple of prusiks; the most popular micro-ascender is the Ropeman. This is rather awkward to fit onto the rope but, once on, is easier to use than a prusik, both to slide and lock on the rope. The Ropeman hinges open and the spring-loaded wheel is clamped onto the rope by clipping a carabiner through the eye. One model has a ridged wheel and is relatively easy to release if required, while the other has tiny sharp teeth and can work with heavier loads. The Ropeman will only slide freely in one direction, shown by an icon on the hinge plate.

The shunt is a versatile piece of equipment that can be used either as a rope ascender or to protect a rappel, with either single or double ropes. However, like the Ropeman, it is quite awkward to fit onto a rope.

A **Ropeman** with ridged wheel—not recommended for heavy shock-loading.

SKYHOOKS

These are hard steel hooks of various sizes that can be balanced on small ledges. They are mainly intended for aid points on artificial climbs, but are actually relatively versatile. On first ascents of climbs with bolt protection that are not pre-equipped by rappelling, a skyhook can allow the leader to use both hands to place a bolt, while on some serious (poorly protected) climbs a skyhook might provide the only semblance of protection.

Pulleys

Pulleys are highly specialized devices for hauling heavy loads. The simplest pulleys consist of a freely rotating wheel between two side plates that clip into a carabiner. The efficient bearings minimize friction when a rope is clipped around the pulley wheel. Very light compromises are now available in the form of a carabiner incorporating a pulley, either as a simple wheel or an integral part of the carabiner. Some pulleys are designed specifically for hauling heavy loads by having a one-way clutch system built in. These include the Wall-hauler and the Traxion or mini-Traxion.

A fixed-plate **pulley**.

Daisy chains

A daisy chain is a sling tied or sewn into a series of segments, any one of which can be clipped to provide an easily adjustable length. Daisy chains are particularly useful for big-wall climbing.

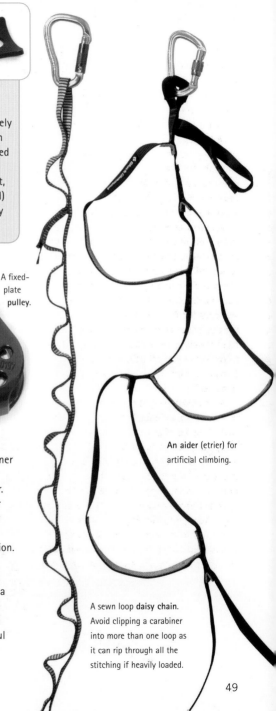

An **aider** (etrier) for artificial climbing.

A sewn loop **daisy chain**. Avoid clipping a carabiner into more than one loop as it can rip through all the stitching if heavily loaded.

KNOTS, BENDS AND HITCHES

Knots and hitches provide the links between the climber, rope and rock, so the ability to recognize and tie them safely is a fundamental skill for roped climbing. Knots are self-sufficient when tied, while a hitch needs to be tied, and remain, around something. A bend connects rope or webbing ends together.

Knots

Overhand (or thumb) knot

This is the simplest of all knots and can be tied using single or multiple strands, or in a bight of rope to form a fixed loop. It tends to pull very tight when loaded, becoming hard to untie and reducing the rope's shock-absorbing potential, so it has limited applications for climbers—apart from its common application (well tightened and with long tails) as the standard knot for connecting two ropes together for rappelling.

Figure-eight knot

Named after its appearance, this is the most versatile of all climbing knots. This is basically an overhand knot with an extra turn around the main rope, making it less prone to overtightening. It is simple to tie, easy to check visually and can perform almost any job that a climber requires from a knot. On the downside, it is bulky and not particularly easy to adjust.

Figure-nine knot

This is a figure-eight knot with yet another turn around the main rope. It is used occasionally when a strong knot is required that is easy to untie after loading.

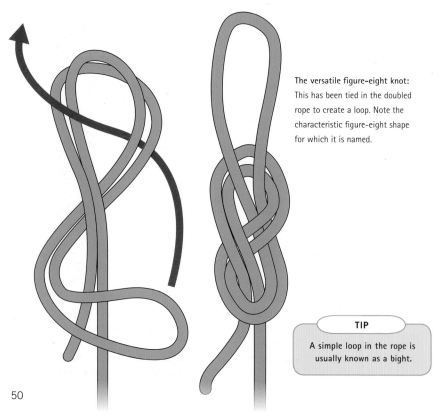

The versatile figure-eight knot:
This has been tied in the doubled rope to create a loop. Note the characteristic figure-eight shape for which it is named.

TIP

A simple loop in the rope is usually known as a bight.

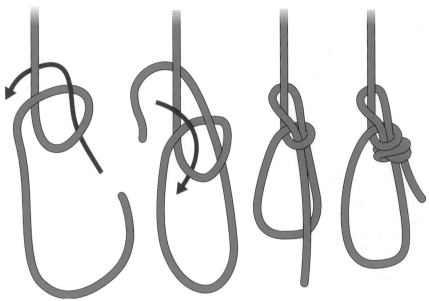

A **bowline knot:** "The rabbit comes out of the hole, goes around the tree, and back down the hole." The end is finished using a stopper knot.

Bowline knot

Another versatile knot, but it is more difficult to learn than the figure-eight knot and unsafe variations are harder to spot. It is also prone to gradually working loose in kernmantle rope, so should always be used in conjunction with a stopper knot and periodically retightened. The bowline knot is used by some experienced climbers for indoor and sport climbing because it is easier to untie after repeated loadings.

Stopper knot

A stopper knot is designed to butt tightly against the main knot to prevent it from working loose. The basic stopper knot is simply an overhand knot tied around the parallel strand of rope, but a more secure double version is commonly used.

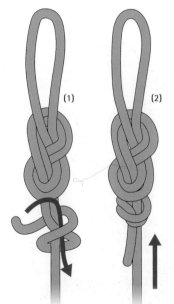

A **double stopper knot:** (1) Wind the end twice around the rope, heading back to the main knot, then feed the end through. (2) Butt against the main knot to prevent slippage.

KNOTS, BENDS AND HITCHES

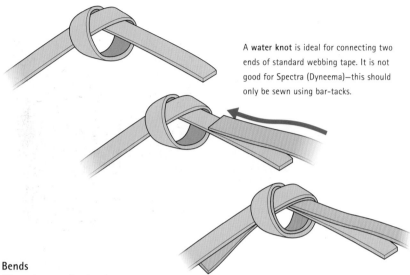

A **water knot** is ideal for connecting two ends of standard webbing tape. It is not good for Spectra (Dyneema)—this should only be sewn using bar-tacks.

Bends
Water knot or ring bend
This is used to connect the ends of a sling into a loop or to link two slings together. It can be used for ropes, too, but the ropes can easily become undone. It is basically an overhand knot in one end, with the other end fed back through in the reverse direction. After tying it should be pulled very tight, with long tail ends (at least five times the sling's width).

Start to form a **clove hitch** as two half hitches, and then cross the hitches on top of each other. Clip the locking carabiner into the looped area.

Hitches
Clove hitch
The clove hitch is secure when fastened tightly but is easy to adjust by pulling open. After adjusting it should always be pulled tight again to prevent it from rolling along the rope when loaded. The clove hitch is used most often to fasten a rope or sling to a carabiner, but it can also be tied onto fence posts or pickets.

Girth hitch

This is a very simple hitch for attaching a sling to a harness or a tree. The sling is simply threaded back through a loop in itself. When attached to a tree or large branch, the sling should be used carefully as it can be very weak in the wrong configuration.

Münter hitch

This hitch capitalizes on the ease with which hitches can be adjusted. It is a non-locking hitch that allows enough friction to provide an excellent belay method when used in conjunction with a locking carabiner, preferably a wide-mouthed (HMS) carabiner. The Münter hitch creates friction by configuring the rope around itself; in practice the heat generated does not melt the nylon when paying out or taking in as no single length is rubbed for more than an instant. However, it is possible that the heat generated by holding a big fall would damage a rope and it is rarely used for belaying lead climbers.

A **girth hitch** is a versatile connection, particularly for connecting a sling to a harness, as in this picture. Avoid clipping a carabiner into the girth hitch as this would just pull the hitch open.

To tie a **Münter hitch**, start as you would for a clove hitch but then fold it over like shutting a book.

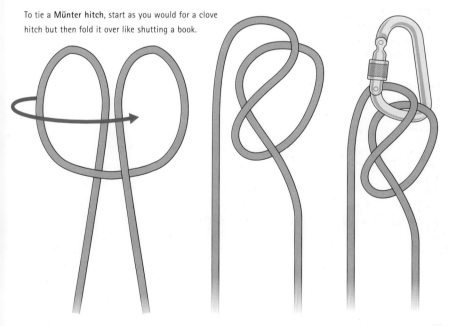

53

TYING IN

To attach yourself to a rope, the first stage is to fit a climbing harness correctly around your legs and waist. The waist belt should feel comfortably snug, and the buckle should be correctly fastened, carefully following the manufacturer's instructions. If the leg loops have adjustable buckles, ensure these are also correctly fastened.

To attach a rope to the harness, a retraced figure-eight knot is normally used; dangle the end of the rope just above the ground and then tie the knot at about waist height. This tail end is then attached to the harness in accordance with the manufacturer's instructions. For most harnesses, the end is threaded through both the waist belt and leg loops of the harness, and then retraced back through the knot. Some lightweight harnesses have a single attachment point and the knot can simply be fastened around

this. The figure-eight knot is retraced in reverse order, so the end goes back through at the point it emerged from the knot nearest to the harness, and then follows back through, keeping exactly parallel to the original rope in the knot.

The completed knot should be pulled tight and have a "tail" end of at least 10 in (25 cm) but not much longer or you will find yourself standing on it. It is normal—but not essential—to tie a stopper knot and butt this up tightly against the figure-eight knot.

Fellow climbers should check each other's harnesses and rope attachment as a matter of routine. If in doubt, discuss the harness and knot with your partner—it may be an unfamiliar knot, but it might be a mistake.

For indoor and sport climbing some people prefer to tie onto the rope using a bowline knot, as it is easier to unfasten after loading.

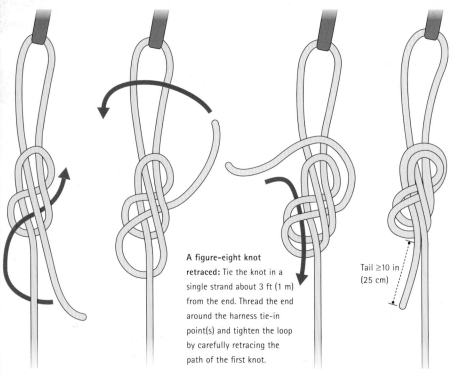

A figure-eight knot retraced: Tie the knot in a single strand about 3 ft (1 m) from the end. Thread the end around the harness tie-in point(s) and tighten the loop by carefully retracing the path of the first knot.

Tail ≥10 in (25 cm)

Below: A climber tied in with a **rethreaded figure-eight knot** and about to butt the stopper knot up against it.

Right: A climber tied in with a **bowline knot**. Finish by butting the stopper knot tightly against the bowline knot.

This should always be used in conjunction with a double stopper knot, as the bowline is prone to inverting when subjected to loading from unusual angles. It is unlikely, but possible, that a bowline knot without a stopper knot could invert and slide undone if the bowline were to snag on something while the climber fell.

It is possible to clip a carabiner to link the rope and harness together. A loop is tied in the rope, usually using a figure-eight knot, and clipped into the carabiner. The carabiner is then clipped into the rappel attachment point on the harness. Note: a carabiner should *never* be clipped into both the leg loop and waist belt as this creates a three-way loading on the carabiner when a third

item—the rope, in this case—is attached. This results in the carabiner being loaded on its weakest axis instead of along the back bar. A carabiner attachment between the rope and climber should in any case be used with great caution. As a compromise, security can be improved by using two locking carabiners with the gates facing in opposing directions. However, it is safer to spend a little longer tying directly into the rope.

TIP

It is always better to ask questions rather than allow an accident to develop simply through reticence.

TYPES OF ANCHOR

An anchor is anything that can be used as a point of attachment to the rock face or the ground. Climbers refer to very secure anchors as "bombproof." Checking anchors calls for a combination of visual checks and directional tugs, requiring practice and judgment. Inexperienced climbers in particular should always err on the side of caution when assessing the suitability of anchors.

A solid **tree anchor**; however, the climber should reposition himself next to the backpack (see page 61).

Trees and bushes

These can usually withstand loading from multiple directions if sturdy and well rooted. Test by a visual inspection and by vigorously shaking the trunk. Unless the tree is exceptionally strong, reduce leverage by attaching to the base of the trunk. Sometimes tree roots emerge from the soil or a crack to form strong threads that may also provide sound anchors.

Boulders

Boulders are detached from the bedrock and vary enormously in scale. They may be buried in soil or lying on the surface. A boulder measuring less than about a cubic yard should be treated with caution as it might not withstand the weight of both climbers if fully loaded. Similarly, beware of boulders—even large ones or those with a buried base—that are precariously poised on a point of balance, or lying on a sloping ledge.

Some boulders are dome-shaped, and will tend to "shrug off" a sling or rope loop when loaded. See if there is an undercut recession at the base into which the loop can be placed. If not, test the stability by running the loop backward and forward around the

boulder—if the loop "rides up" and off the boulder, the anchor is not safe. If a domed boulder seems usable, try to keep the loading point lower than the base of the boulder if possible.

Spikes and flakes

These terms refer to a finger or sliver of rock, usually attached to bedrock and ideally pointing away from the direction of loading. Test first with a visual check for fractures or crumbling, and then with a firm slap, watching and feeling for vibration or movement. A freestanding spike or flake should be treated in the same way as a

> **TIP**
>
> Test likely boulders with a hefty slap or kick—being careful not to knock it onto anybody—and watch carefully for any movement.

When placing a sling over a large solid spike, **reduce leverage** by seating the sling at the base of the spike.

can provide excellent anchors if the stopper is firmly seated. Piled blocks or boulders may be threaded if there is space between them, but check the blocks are firmly wedged and the connecting area does not crumble.

Cracks

Wires, hexes and cams may all be used for anchors and are described in more detail on page 82. Ensure the placement will work for the anticipated load direction: a wire that will only resist a downward pull, for example, is of little use for a sideways pull. Some cracks, notably hairline fissures, might only accept pitons.

boulder. Virtually any size of spike or flake from about ½ in (1 cm) upward can be utilized, but only if the rock is tough enough and the rope/tape loop is not prone to sliding off of its "shoulders."

Pockets

A simple hole in the rock might provide an anchor if it is wedge-shaped (so allowing a nut to be placed) or slot-shaped (allowing a cramming device to be deployed). Some shallow pockets might allow a sideways wire placement, and a small but deep hole might just allow a piton to be inserted. Pitons are best left in place, as removal damages the rock.

Threads

It may be possible to thread a hole in the rock face with rope or webbing to give an anchor that can resist loading in multiple directions. Some threads are formed by a block jammed in a crack, known as a natural stopper. These

CONSTRUCTING SAFE BELAYS

The forces involved in roped falls
Understanding the potential forces involved in roped climbing will help you set up realistic belay anchors. A person weighing about 220 lb (100 kg) exerts a force of 220 lb or 1 kilonewton (kN) just by hanging on the end of a rope; this can double if they are bouncing around, say while rappelling. If that person climbed a few yards and fell off before the slack rope was taken in, this would create an impact force of perhaps 900 lb (4 kN). A high impact force is a large force applied over a short time period—such a force can have a greater effect than a lower force applied over a proportionally longer time period.

A belay system set up for belaying climbers from above (top-rope belaying) needs to be able to withstand a potential impact force of 900 lb (4 kN) if low-stretch ropes are used. A system for lead climbing needs to be able to withstand much larger forces because the rate of deceleration is much greater after a lengthy fall. If our same climber above took a 60 ft (18 m) fall and was suddenly halted, the impact force could be enormous, maybe 3,400 lb (15 kN). This would be enough to shatter most items of climbing equipment, and would also break the climber's bones. The reason this does not happen is mainly because we use dynamic ropes for lead climbing. Because the rope stretches, the impact force is spread over time due to the gradual deceleration. Thin ropes with a lower impact rating actually put less strain on anchors than stronger ropes.

The safety chain
This includes every element of a belay system. The rope, knots, harnesses, anchors, rock crystals, belay device and even friction

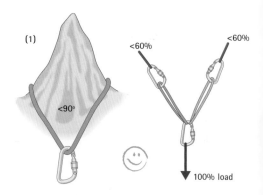

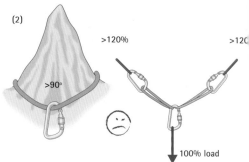

Optimal angles between two anchor points and the load: (1) Less than 60°: each anchor takes about 50 percent of the load. (2) More than 120°: each anchor takes more load than a single anchor would. Bombproof anchors required.

all play a part in absorbing the energy of a fall. The safety chain is only as strong as its weakest link: if that fails, the rest of the chain, however strong, collapses. Because a climber's body can only withstand a maximum of about 2,250 lb (10 kN) without serious internal injuries, there is little point in the harness being much stronger than this.

The top anchor is subjected to a pulley effect: the sum of both the impact force on one side and the belaying force on the other. Friction on the top carabiner absorbs some of the belay force, so the top anchor is loaded by around 1.6 times the force on the climber

IMPACT FORCE RATINGS OF TYPICAL ITEMS OF EQUIPMENT

Item	Rating in lb	Rating in kN
½ in (11 mm) rope	2,090	9.2
Locking carabiner	4,950	21.8
¼ in (6 mm) cord	1,500	6.6
²/₅ in (10 mm) x 2½ in (60 mm) bolt	4,000	17.6
Medium wired nut or cam	2,700	12.0
⁹/₁₆ in (14 mm) Spectra tape	6,075	26.7

Three ways to equalize anchors using a sling or cordelette:
(1) Tie an overhand knot to create the equivalent of two slings. Clip both loops.
(2) Clip all three and tie a big knot to create fixed loops.
(3) Clove hitch anchors and overhand knot for loop.

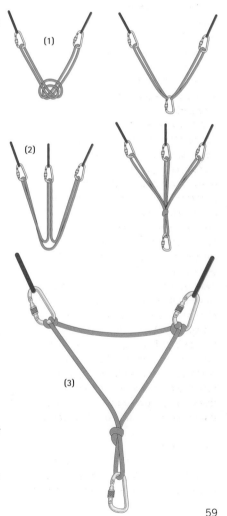

in total. In practice, rope slippage through the belay device reduces this and friction from protection located out to the sides increases it, but either way the impact force can certainly be enough to break micro-wires and rip small wires and cams out as rock crystal disintegrates. Research suggests that in real situations the maximum impact force that can be generated is about 3,000 lb (13 kN) and the minimum about 680 lb (3 kN), so items rated at less than 680 lb (3 kN) cannot survive a leader fall intact.

Fall factors

The more rope there is between the faller and the belayer, the more energy can be absorbed by the rope. The impact force felt by the climber when top-roping gets progressively greater as the belay is approached, whereas for a lead climber the impact force actually decreases as the rope pays out—if the lead climber is placing good protection on the way. The length of a fall divided by the length of rope available to absorb it is known as the fall factor. Thus a 30 ft (9 m) lead fall from 150 ft (48 m) up a pitch results in a fall factor of 0.2 (30÷150). This gives low impact forces and little stress on the equipment. Contrast this with a leader falling from 3 ft (1 m) up a pitch before placing protection. The resulting 6 ft (2 m) fall gives a fall factor of 2 (6÷3). This stresses the equipment, the belay and the climber.

CONSTRUCTING SAFE BELAYS

A belay needs to be able to comfortably withstand any potential impact force from a fall, so climbers should work according to sound engineering principles when constructing them.

The START system
Give your belay a good START—this is a simple mnemonic that can help reinforce the principles behind sound belays.

- **Simple:** Minimize the amount of equipment and make it easy to adjust. A clove-hitched sling is better than a quickdraw on both counts.
- **Tested:** Are the anchors as good as they look? Test them!
- **Angle:** Diagonal loads create vector forces that multiply the effect of the

Types of in situ (already in place) anchors:
(1) Thread and (2) Spike—both natural.
(3) Stake and (4) Piton or bolt—both constructed.

load. The optimum angle between anchor connections is 60°. This gives stability without compromising strength. Angles beyond 120° create such large vector forces that the load on each anchor is greater than if only one of the anchors was used!

- **Reliance:** No element should rely entirely on another—otherwise, if one fails, all fail. Each element should therefore be independently secured so that failure of one does not cause shock-loading of another. Avoid relying on any one element: think about each item and provide something to take over if it should fail. Even a single bombproof anchor would benefit from double slings and carabiners.
- **Tensioned:** Keep everything tensioned so that individual elements do not get shock-loaded in the event of a fall. Adjust distances so that each anchor is taking part of the load.

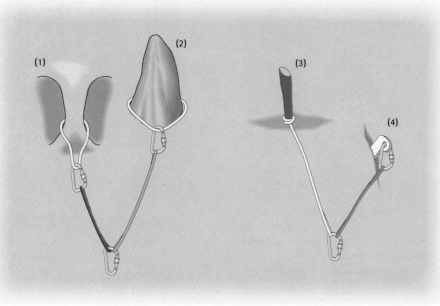

The ABC principle in use: This belayer is positioned directly below her anchor and directly above her climbing partner.

The ABC principle

A belay should be set up so that the anchor point, belayer and climber line up with each other vertically. When loaded due to a fall, the force on the rope naturally pulls all three into line, so it's best to start there in order to fulfill our "angle" and "tension" principles. This has several implications. For top-rope belaying, the anchor is best located directly above the hardest moves if the line wanders. For anchors that are lower than waist level, the belayer's knees would tend to buckle,

One rope used to equalize two anchors that are within arm's reach: A clove hitch attaches the rope tightly to the thread anchor. Another clove hitch attaches the other anchor, and this is tied back to the harness rope loop. The clove hitches allow easy adjustments.

CONSTRUCTING SAFE BELAYS

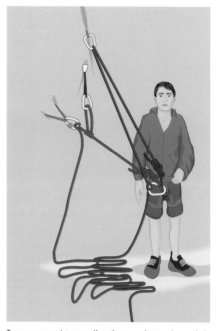

One rope used to equalize two anchors that are out of reach: Clip the rope through both then pull the rope between them back to your harness. Tie off the resulting loops to a carabiner or two attached to your harness.

Two ropes used to equalize three anchors using a tied-off loop for one and a knot on a bight plus a clove hitch for the two closer anchors.

so it's best to sit or use a direct belay. Finally, a climb up the crest of a promontory can be problematic as a falling second could pull the belayer around the arête. This is one case where anchors far out to either side can be very useful to help prevent a pendulum, especially if combined with a sitting stance.

Ways to share the load

- **Webbing loop:** Anchors can be equalized using webbing or rope. A webbing loop some 4 ft (1.2 m) long can be used to equally load two anchors that are up to about an arm's length apart. The basic principle is to choose a method that brings the two sides in at an angle of 90° or less. A simple and effective way is to tie an overhand knot somewhere near the middle of the webbing, and clip each end into anchors. Manipulate the knot over until the anticipated load is shared between both anchors. Clip the equalizing carabiner into each side of the knot as if that was a separate loop. An alternative is to simply use two separate slings, but beware that three-way loading on the carabiner could cause impact force to be directed onto the gate; this can be avoided by tying a big knot around both slings and clipping in beyond this. There are several other methods of equalizing anchors but beware of so-called equalizing triangles that allow shock-loading if one of the two anchors should fail.

- **Cordelette:** A loop of cord or thin webbing around 8 ft (2.4 m) long can be used to

American mountain guide John Bicknell has used **webbing** to equalize two good anchors for a hanging belay on the Red Rocks classic, A Dream of Wild Turkeys (5.10a).

equalize several anchors if they are fairly close together. Clip the anchors and bring the linking cord down to form a series of loops. Equalize these, then tie a huge overhand knot around the whole thing. The resulting loop is strong and shares the load effectively.

- **The lead rope:** The climbing rope can be used in many ways to share the load. A useful method to equalize anchors that are a long way back from the best place to stand is to make the tension adjustments at the harness. The rope is clipped into an anchor carabiner, and brought back to the harness. A carabiner is clipped into the harness attachment loop and the rope is clove-hitched to this, allowing easy adjustments. The rope emerging from this is clipped to another anchor and brought back to the harness in the same way. If a wide-mouthed (HMS) carabiner is used, two clove hitches can be conveniently accommodated on the same carabiner.

- **Other methods:** If all the anchors are aligned with the direction of loading, they can be simply equalized with a series of clove hitches. However, if these anchors all utilize the same crack, check it cannot expand, otherwise this fails our "reliance" principle.

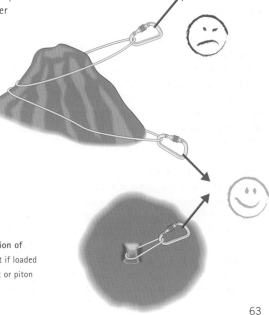

Think carefully about the anticipated **direction of loading**. Spikes, wires and cams may lift out if loaded in the wrong direction. A sound thread, bolt or piton can normally be loaded in any direction.

BELAY METHODS

To safeguard a climber using the rope, the belayer must be able to pay out or take in the rope steadily, but be ready to lock the rope in the event of a fall. This requires skillful rope handling and constant attention. Normally, specialized equipment is used to create this adjustable system. The rope between the climber and the belay device is called the "live" rope, and the rope beyond the device is used for braking, so this will be referred to as the "brake" rope.

Direct belays

With direct belays the belay device is attached directly to the anchor. With bombproof anchors this is a convenient way of belaying the second climber, or top-roping.

The Münter hitch

It is definitely worth learning to tie the Münter hitch, which is a more suitable belaying method for direct belays than using a normal belay plate. Although the Münter hitch creates friction on the rope, in practical use the heat does not melt the rope because any length of rope is only subject to friction for a second. Having said that, it is possible that using a Münter hitch to hold a big fall could generate enough friction to cause damage to the rope.

The Münter hitch is simple to tie: start to form a clove hitch as two half hitches, then fold the hitches on top of each other instead of passing one behind the other as you would to finish the clove hitch.

> **TIP**
>
> The Münter hitch creates more friction when the brake end of the rope is held in front of the belay, unlike belay devices, which must be pulled back. The Münter hitch should be used in direct belay situations where the belayer is standing closer to the cliff edge than to the belay device.

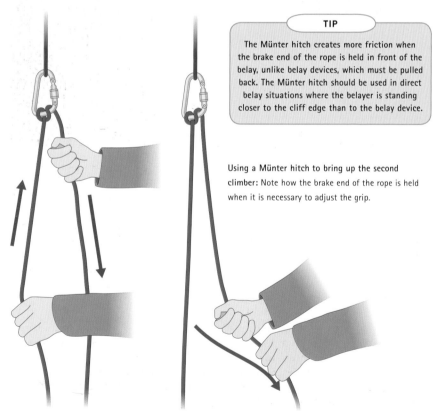

Using a Münter hitch to bring up the second climber: Note how the brake end of the rope is held when it is necessary to adjust the grip.

An HMS (pear-shaped) carabiner is then clipped into the looped area. Another way to tie the hitch is by wrapping a bight of rope around a length of the rope and clipping the carabiner onto the parallel pieces of rope. Once learned, this method is simple to remember.

The Reverso and other "magic" plates
Some belay devices are designed to function both as a normal "indirect" belay device for safeguarding a leader and as a direct belay device for bringing up one or two climbers on independent ropes. The normal belay mode functions much like any other plate, but the device incorporates a second carabiner and vertical alignment in direct belay mode

Using a solid spike to create sufficient friction for a direct belay: This is a fast technique but only appropriate for long, easy climbs.

(see page 89). The second carabiner is clipped through the rope loop and traps the brake rope against the plate when the live rope is loaded, so this system, like the grigri, is self-locking when used correctly.

Simple friction
On easy ground a solid and prominent spike can be used for belaying by means of a single wrap of the rope. With experience, the amount of friction can be varied, but this method is harsh on the rope, and demands good judgment.

BELAY METHODS

Indirect belays

In indirect belays the belay device is connected to the belayer rather than directly to the anchor.

Belay plates and similar gadgets

These are generally the most popular belay devices: the rope passes through the device in a "Z" shape. Retaining this shape demands some care when taking in, particularly when swapping hands on the brake end of the rope in order to slide the belaying hand closer to the plate. A rhythm should be developed to take in slack rope efficiently. When holding a fall, or simply "weighting" the rope, the plate is automatically pulled closer to the carabiner, tightening the bends and thus increasing the holding power.

A belay plate clipped to the belayer's harness should ideally be used with the belayer positioned sideways to the climb; this allows the belaying hand to be pulled backward without being restricted by the belayer's hip. Similarly, when tying

> **TIP**
>
> If the belay device keeps "snatching" so that it is difficult to pay the rope out, fix an extra carabiner between the strands of rope in the belay carabiner.

(1)
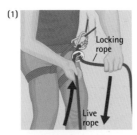
Locking rope
Live rope

(2)
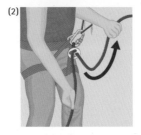

(3)
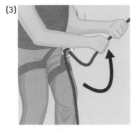

(4)
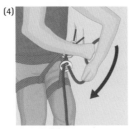

(5)
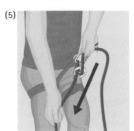

Taking in slack rope using a belay plate: (1) Feed and pull rope through the plate by pushing the brake hand toward the climber. (2) Pull the brake hand back to lock the device. (3) Share hands on the braking end of the rope. (4) Move the brake hand back toward the plate. (5) Repeat.

in to a belay, the rope(s) will pass over one of the belayer's hips. The brake hand should be on this same side, so the hand can be pulled back without hitting the hip. However, this is often hard to do when using a constricted stance, as the rock gets in the way. You should be aware, though, that a departure from these guidelines will always make it more difficult to hold a fall.

The grigri

This device is best used for sport climbing and top-roping, because it locks immediately and creates a bigger impact force on the top anchor than other belay methods, all of which allow a more gradual deceleration. The problem for belayers is that trying to yank the rope out quickly usually causes the device to lock up. Careful anticipation will allow the belayer to pay rope out once the leader has placed a quickdraw and is about to pull rope up to clip in.

It helps to stand back a little from the rock face, so that by stepping forward, considerably more rope

Feeding the rope into a grigri: (1) The live rope should emerge from next to the carabiner hole. Note the etched reminder on the hinged cover. (2) Try to anticipate when the leader will require more rope. (3) A common error: The braking rope end should pass over the rounded side plate as in the previous picture, to reduce wear on plastic parts.

becomes available for the leader to use, even if the device jams up by pulling the rope too hard. There have been instances of belayers failing to hold a fall when the leader has fallen while pulling up rope to clip protection. This is because squeezing the device to pull out rope quickly will prevent the locking mechanism from working, and there may not be enough time to recover from this while the leader is airborne.

To lower somebody back down a climb, a grip should be kept on the brake end of the rope while the plastic lever is pulled back to reduce the holding power. The grigri can also be used for direct belays.

The waist belay
The waist belay is the original belay method but is now rarely used in rock climbing because it is likely to result in friction burns when loaded. It can, however,

Using a waist belay correctly: The rope can be wrapped around the locking arm. The attachment to the anchor should be on the same side of the body as the live rope to prevent body rotation. Note the protective glove for the brake hand.

be useful for experienced climbers on easy ground if speed is of the essence.

The waist belay is a dynamic system, so rope can be allowed to slip through and gradually be brought to a halt. Taking in slack rope is effected by holding both the live and brake rope in the live hand and sliding the brake hand back to the waist to pull in the slack. As with all belay methods, the brake hand should remain cupped around the rope at all times in order to react immediately in the event of the climber falling while the rope is being taken in.

TOP-ROPING SAFELY

Top-roping a pitch allows climbers to tackle a route without worrying unduly about the consequences of a fall. Top-roping is an important ingredient of a team ascent of multi-pitch climbs, as only one person needs to lead each pitch; any other members of the party gain a top-rope to second the pitch. On most single-pitch routes, leading is optional as it is usually possible to walk around to the top of the pitch in order to establish a belay station. Often a climber will lead an easier pitch and then arrange a top-rope nearby to tackle a harder neighboring route.

Some climbing gyms have areas set up for top-roping, with ropes already threaded through anchor points at the top of the wall. These may be steel bars or, more often, a couple of bolts linked by a chain to give a single anchor point, which should be a locked carabiner. The usual arrangement is for the belayer to stand at the bottom of the wall, with the rope running up the wall, through the anchor point, and back down to the climber (slingshot top-roping).

The basic safety checks are the same for any top-roping activity. Avoid distractions at a busy venue, confirm each other's harnesses are properly fastened and that the rope is correctly attached to the climber's harness. Check the rope has not snagged on some projection on the rock face—if necessary, flick the rope until it travels freely. Thread the rope carefully into the belay device and make sure the belayer is able to lock it correctly.

Standard top-rope belay

If the belayer is going to operate at the top of the crag, the main system choices are:

Direct belay
The belay device is attached directly to an equalized anchor point. If the anchors are close together, slings can be used to equalize. If they are further apart, the rope is used to link them, or possibly a separate "rigging" rope brought especially for this purpose is used. The rope can be looped through several anchors and brought to a convenient point for belaying. Having equalized all the loops, everything—including the single strands—can be tied off in one huge overhand knot to create a bundle of loops, any or all of which can be clipped as an equalized central point.

The belayer can be attached to the central point by a longer leash, usually a sling attached by a girth hitch to the harness.

> **TIP**
>
> For indoor climbs, at the top of the wall make sure the climber does not unclip the top carabiner by mistake, then check communication and lower the climber back down.

The **attentive belayer** on the right will not be pulled off balance by a fall. The other belayer is watching the wrong person and standing too far to one side, risking an inability to hold a fall.

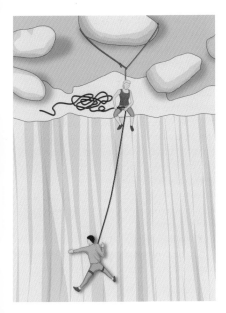

The belayer above is attached to **a good anchor** and is belaying from her harness. This is a typical system used to bring up a climber after leading a pitch.

The belayer below has **a good view** down the climb. The belay device is clipped to a rope loop rather than her harness: A Münter hitch would be easier to lock in this situation.

COMMUNICATION

Climbers have developed a simple communications system of clear calls that can be heard against background noise in normal circumstances. The classic climbing calls relate to the sequence of setting up a belay and preparing to climb. The calls and their meanings are as follows:

Leader: "Off belay!" or "Safe!" *I have set up a belay and you can now release the rope from the belay plate.*
Second: "Rope's free!" or "Belay off!" *The rope is no longer belayed so you can take in the slack.*
Leader: "Taking in!" *I will pull up all the spare rope.*
Second: "That's me!" *The rope is now tight onto my harness.*
Leader: "Belay on!" *I have you on belay so you can start climbing.*
Second: "Climbing!" *From now on I won't be connected to anchors, so take in any slack.*
Leader: "Climb" or "OK!" (optional) *Message understood. Start climbing.*

While climbing up the pitch, some simple unambiguous instructions can also be very useful and might be used by either the leader or the second:

"Up rope!" *The rope isn't tight enough. Pull the slack back through the belay device.*
"Slack!" *The rope is too tight. Pay out some slack.*

Any variations on the above calls are bound to confuse in windy conditions when only one half of the call is heard. A climber must soon learn how to project their voice over background noise. Of course, on a windless day with short pitches, it may be feasible to conduct a normal conversation. At other times, if it is impossible to hear anything, a predetermined sequence of tugs must be arranged.

TOP-ROPING SAFELY

Ensure the belayer is able to lock the device properly—a Münter hitch can be locked from any direction and is generally the best choice for direct belays.

Indirect belay

This is basically the same as the system often used when a lead climber brings up the second. The belayer is tied to the anchors or a central point and the belay device is operated from the harness belay point. Any loading is shared between the belayer and the anchor. For a group top-roping session, this method is less convenient for the belayer.

Slingshot top-roping

The rope is passed through a carabiner attached to an anchor point at the top of a pitch, which acts as a pulley above the belayer handling the rope on one side, and the climber attached to the rope on the other. Slingshot top-roping can potentially result in considerable friction if the rope passes over the top of the crag, causing damage to both the rope and the rock that can be avoided. Some crags have bolts just below the top. This sometimes requires the rope to be threaded through two bolts (or a chain and ring connecting them), but often the bolts are linked to a single ring or locking carabiner. Be very careful at the edge of the crag; it is best to wear a harness and be clipped to an anchor before the final approach.

If the anchors are set back from the edge, it is necessary to create a central attachment point and then extend this over the crag

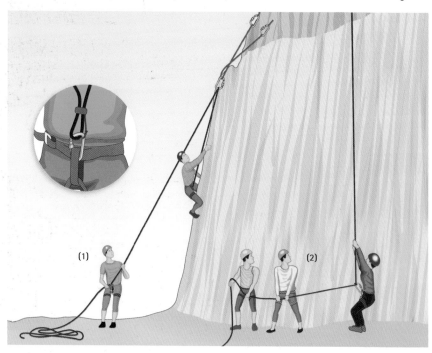

Slingshot top-roping by an individual climber (1) and by a group (2). The group is using a direct body belay with a Münter hitch and several people handle the rope, keeping more novices occupied and providing a failsafe belayer. The individual is using a belay device in the normal way (see inset).

When **slingshot top-roping**, keep the rope tight especially for the first few feet of the climb as the rope will stretch if loaded heavily.

edge using extra webbing or rope. Because the belay point is unattended, it is best to use two locking carabiners or a fixed ring (for example, a figure-eight descender attached to the loop with a girth hitch through the smaller ring).

The belayer should stand directly underneath the anchor station to avoid being pulled off balance. As the climber embarks on the pitch, the belayer takes in any slack rope as it appears. The rope may be clipped through a few pieces of protection if the route is overhanging or takes a wandering line; these will need to be unclipped as the climber passes them, and then reclipped on the descent for the next climber.

This climber has reached the top of the climb and is being lowered back to the ground using a **slingshot top-roping system**. Note the doubled locking carabiners for extra safety.

BELAYING PROCEDURES FOR LEAD CLIMBING OUTDOORS

Belaying is an integrated system comprising communications, anchor choice and attachments, appropriate use of a belay device and rope, and correct location of the belayer relative to the climber. Safe belaying is fundamental to roped climbing because the rope is attached for the sole purpose of allowing a belay to be provided.

Setting up a belay station

A belay station is the point of attachment to the rock face where the system for protecting the roped climber is located. This may be a ground anchor, but more often it is situated at the top of a pitch. For single-pitch climbs, a top station simply needs to be able to withstand downward loading. On climbs with more than one pitch the belay station might have to withstand loading from below, sideways or even from above if a heavy leader falls and pulls the belayer up from the stance.

Before setting up any belay system you should take a moment to consider the likely direction of loading if a fall should occur. The belay station for bringing somebody up from below should be chosen in a position that ideally is directly above the climb, or at least above the hardest part of the climb.

Fall factors: The available rope has to absorb all of the energy. So 30 ft (9 m) of rope will be more severely tested in Example 1.

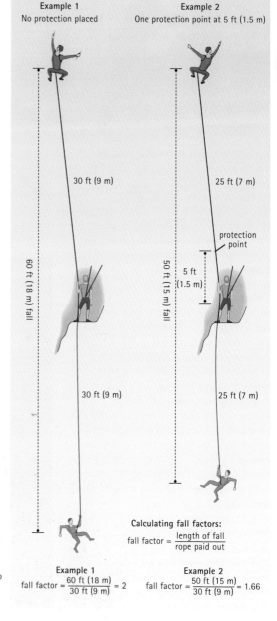

Example 1
No protection placed

30 ft (9 m)

60 ft (18 m) fall

30 ft (9 m)

Example 2
One protection point at 5 ft (1.5 m)

25 ft (7 m)

protection point

50 ft (15 m) fall

5 ft (1.5 m)

25 ft (7 m)

Calculating fall factors:

$$\text{fall factor} = \frac{\text{length of fall}}{\text{rope paid out}}$$

Example 1
$$\text{fall factor} = \frac{60 \text{ ft } (18 \text{ m})}{30 \text{ ft } (9 \text{ m})} = 2$$

Example 2
$$\text{fall factor} = \frac{50 \text{ ft } (15 \text{ m})}{30 \text{ ft } (9 \text{ m})} = 1.66$$

Lead climbing

Single-pitch climbs

If the lead climber is considerably heavier than the belayer, a ground anchor might be advisable to protect the belayer in the event of a fall. Awkward terrain at the foot of the climb can also make this a sensible precaution. The leader places protection along the way and should try to minimize rope drag, because friction impedes progress and increases the potential impact force. Placements far out to the side should be extended with a longer sling. At the top of the pitch the leader constructs a belay and normally uses an indirect belay to safeguard the second climber. For some short pitches the belay comprises a lowering station so the leader can descend in order to slingshot top-rope.

The ideal stance has high anchors and allows the lead climber to stand near the cliff edge so that communication with the second climber is excellent. If the anchors are low, the best solution is usually to sit near the edge. Some cliffs have domed summits and communication is poor, so any instructions are best

given before disappearing out of sight.

Multi-pitch climbs

Multi-pitch climbs require at least one intermediate belay before the top of the crag is reached. The climbing team will either need to swap over belayers at the stance if the same person is leading all the pitches, or swap leaders. The belay anchors need to be able to withstand loading first from below, and then from the pitch above.

It is normally simpler for the person who seconds a pitch to lead on up the pitch above if appropriate. On arrival at the stance, the climber clips into an anchor point (preferably an equalized one) and for added security the belayer might tie a knot in the rope beyond the belay device. The climber rearranges all the protection equipment for efficient deployment and prepares to embark on the next pitch. Finally, the temporary sling and backup knot are removed and the new leader sets off up the next pitch.

The leader should endeavor to place protection as soon as possible after leaving the stance to prevent subjecting the belay to fall factor 2 forces in the event of a fall. If this is not possible, clipping the rope through an extender onto the highest anchor in the belay system will reduce the fall factor as long as the anchor is good enough to take the pulley effect (as any belay anchor should).

Several pitches up a long climb, the belayer **safeguards her partner** as she battles with the crux, security supplied by the rope passing through pieces of protection.

LEARNING TO LEAD

Once you have completed plenty of climbs on a top-rope you may wish to progress to leading. This is not a decision to make lightly, because there are potentially high penalties to be paid for mistakes. Leading a climb can feel terribly lonely; when contemplating a fall is not the moment to realize that you don't trust your ability to fasten anchors.

Leading a climb requires three sets of skills: the technical ability to "read" the moves and perform them, the confidence to climb above protection and cope with the

heightened sense of exposure, and the craft of finding anchors and constructing safe belays. These skills must all be built on experience—confidence must be built on successful experiments rather than blind faith.

Sport climbing

Bolts eliminate much of the craft required in placing protection, allowing novice leaders to progress with more confidence, particularly at a climbing gym where the vagaries of damp and loose holds should be eliminated.

A climbing gym is an excellent venue for your first lead, giving you the thrill of moving above protection and trusting your partner's belaying ability. Ensure that your partner can belay competently and hold falls, and discipline yourselves to run through the normal attachment checks. The techniques required for leading sport climbs are described more fully in the following pages.

Traditional climbing

A longer apprenticeship is required in order to fully understand how natural protection works. The craft of arranging natural protection brings a dimension to climbing that many people find richly rewarding. For others, the concentration required to examine the rock for potential protection placements is a distraction from the real issue, which is movement.

What do you do if you can't get to a sports crag but don't trust your gear placements? Practice placing protection equipment at ground level and tug it in various directions to see what happens. This sort of exercise can sharpen up your observational skills for traditional leads, while remaining in a relatively safe environment.

Leading on a climbing wall: Bolted climbs provide a safer learning environment for novice lead climbers than traditional routes, as natural protection can fail if not skillfully placed.

Leading on multi-pitch climbs like this requires plenty of practice in setting up belays. Remember the belayer may be pulled upward if the leader falls off of the next pitch, so arrange high and multi-directional anchors.

TIP

You may find it reassuring to make your first leads on routes that you have previously top-roped.

A mock lead can be a good introduction; top-rope the route trailing a spare rope and placing protection on the way. A more realistic temporary "sport route" can be made without bolts. Arrange a good belay at the top of the pitch and attach a spare rope to dangle down the climb. Attach a series of loops using overhand knots, and attach quickdraws as pieces of protection. You can supplement them with natural protection and get feedback from your partner.

Hanging on to the rock face while placing protection requires a lot more stamina than clipping bolts. Use ledges, large holds and comfortable jams to place good protection,

then spot the next rest point and head straight to it. Don't tug on placements to test them unless you have a good hold for the other hand.

Multi-pitch climbs

You should gain confidence leading single-pitch climbs before venturing onto multi-pitch leads, where escaping from a crag can be much more difficult if things don't go according to plan. A leader falling from above a belay has the potential to load the belay system with a fall factor 2, which can severely test the anchors and the belayer.

USING FIXED PROTECTION AND QUICKDRAWS

Fixed equipment is by no means limited to sport climbs. All fixed equipment requires the climber to make a judgment about the stability of the placement. Look for signs of corrosion and cracks or crumbling in the surrounding rock. Metalware such as pitons and bolts should ideally have their heads flush with the rock for minimum leverage. Failing this, a sling can be attached using a clove or girth hitch. Threaded cord or webbing can also provide fixed protection on both sport and traditional climbs. A thread may have been used for retreating, and if no carabiner has been left, this will have caused friction damage when the rope was retrieved. Look out for abrasion or bleaching, as these are visible signs of deterioration.

Most fixed equipment is best clipped with a quickdraw or even a longer sling in order to reduce

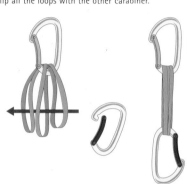

An extendable quickdraw: Feed the sling end part way through the carabiner to make three loops and clip all the loops with the other carabiner.

friction—which both impedes a leader's progress and increases impact forces on the climber and top protection point in a fall (see *Constructing Safe Belays* on page 58). Some threads may be long enough simply to clip directly with a carabiner.

Some pitons are hammered into cracks at the back of narrow ledges, where the carabiner is likely to lever the piton up and out. This tendency can be eliminated by threading a sling through the eye and clipping it into the doubled ends.

Left: **A knife blade piton.** Note how this was not hammered fully home, requiring a subjective appraisal of its holding power.

Right: **A small thread anchor.** Check that the webbing is not cut or badly abraded.

An expansion bolt: Check that the nut is reasonably tight and the metal is not badly corroded. Look out for fractures in the rock as well.

Left: **A sling** has been threaded through the eye of this piton as there was not room for a carabiner. The piton above feels loose so has not been used.

Right: Using a **stick clip** to preclip a high first bolt and thus prevent a nasty ground fall.

Below: **Clipping a carabiner** correctly. The rope should pass from between the rock and the carabiner outward, so that in the event of a fall the rope will not loop over the gate and unclip.

Sometimes it may be convenient to clip fixed equipment with a single carabiner if this does not create significant rope drag, but avoid clipping two carabiners together as an extension. The minimal reduction in friction is counterbalanced by a high risk that they will twist in a fall and lever a gate open, so use an extender sling. Quickdraws are generally best arranged with both carabiner gates facing in the same direction, then attached to protection so that the carabiner back bars are in contact with the rock rather than the gates. Occasionally this will require one of the carabiners to be turned to face the opposite direction. The gate of the bottom carabiner on the quickdraw should ideally face away from the direction the climber is traveling in so that a fall would bring the rope over the back bar rather than the gate.

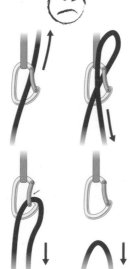

> **TIP**
>
> For hard moves near the ground consider using locking carabiners linked by an extension sling on the first bolt, or preclipping the first bolt or two using an extendable clip stick to prevent a possible ankle-breaking ground fall.

When the rope is clipped through an extender, it is important that the live rope emerges in front of the carabiner. This significantly reduces the likelihood of the quickdraw being twisted by friction and either becoming unclipped, or the top carabiner's gate being forced open and releasing from either the protection or the rope.

SPORT CLIMBING SAFELY

Climbing gyms are much less intimidating than natural crags. The relaxed and sociable atmosphere makes the whole thing seem very cozy and safe, so much so that accidents at climbing gyms can occur due to careless mistakes.

Clipping the rope

Clipping the rope into a quickdraw is an important skill that gets easier with practice. The carabiner should be hanging with the opening end of the gate downward; this makes it easier to clip the rope in. The rope should travel through the carabiner in the same direction that you are moving, so if a step left follows the clip, the carabiner gate should face right and the rope be clipped from behind the carabiner. In the event of a fall this prevents a rope loop from snagging on the gate and unclipping as a result.

A gently overhanging wall is an ideal place to **practice falling safely**. Note the upright and relaxed posture of the falling climber.

You can either stand below the protection point and pull up sufficient rope to clip in above your head, or you can climb boldly on until the bolt is just below your waist, and reach down to clip it. An attentive belayer is essential because pulling the rope to clip protection is the most vulnerable moment.

At the top of the wall, clip the final carabiner and make sure your partner has taken in any slack rope before allowing yourself to be lowered. If you decide to screw the gate shut for extra security, don't crank it too tight when hanging from it, because on release of tension the metal contracts and locks tightly. Some climbing gyms have a snapgate carabiner attached to the same anchor to allow a quick clip if this happens.

For sport climbs on outdoor crags you will have to contend with other factors, such as the climate and its effects on the rock. Don't start leading outdoors until you've learned to test holds and never take fixed protection for granted. It is a good idea to get a more experienced leader to preclip quickdraws into the bolts, but otherwise count the number of quickdraws required and carry this number plus a couple extra for hidden bolts and the top station. Be very careful around the first two protection points as a slip from this height can easily cause a ground fall.

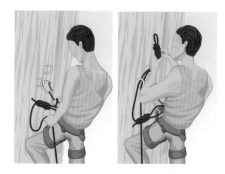

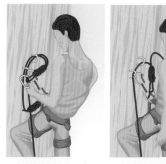

Threading fixed rings at a belay station: Attach your harness to the anchor(s) using quickdraws. Feed a loop of rope through the anchor(s), tie a knot on the loop and clip this to the harness belay loop. Untie the original end, pull it free and check with tension from the belayer before removing quickdraws.

Most outdoor sport climbs have a much less convenient arrangement at the top of the pitch. Generally there will be two bolts to provide a failsafe in the event of a bolt failure. Often, staples or eco-bolts are used. The rope must be threaded through both bolts to allow a lower-off. One method of achieving this is to clip your harness rappel loop into both bolts. Next, pull up some slack rope and tie a clove hitch; clip this into your harness. You can now untie from the rope without fear of dropping it, feed the rope through both bolts, and tie back into the rope. Get your partner to take in the slack, double-check, then unclip the quickdraws and allow yourself to be lowered.

Alternatively, clip into one bolt and pull up enough slack rope to thread a loop through both. Tie an overhand or figure-eight knot into the loop and clip this to your rappel loop with one or two locking carabiners. Get your partner to take in the slack until you can feel the pull. After a double-check, untie your original attachment and pull the slack end through the bolts. The rope now passes from the belayer, up the climb and through both bolts to a knot attached to your harness. All that is left is to unclip the quickdraw and allow your partner to lower you to the ground.

A high first anchor: Consider carrying a few wires to protect the intermediate moves or preclip the bolt using a stick clip.

> **TIP**
>
> Practice rethreading anchors near ground level so that you do not drop the rope or get the sequence wrong while high above the ground.

PLACING AND REMOVING PROTECTION

Natural protection

Before metal wedges and camming devices were developed, natural protection was limited to spikes and threads, with the later addition of pebbles hand-placed in cracks to allow thread placements. This latter technique has of course been superseded, but spikes and threads remain important choices.

Long slings are very versatile, both for protection and equalizing anchors. Slings measuring 4 ft (1.2 m) can be carried doubled around the neck with one twist, and then a locking carabiner fastened to both ends. The twist stops the carabiner from falling off if the sling is pulled off over the head. The easiest way to deploy the sling is to unclip the carabiner from one end and pull the sling free.

Using threads and spikes

Threads and spikes were discussed as potential belays earlier, but utilizing them for

> **TIP**
>
> A sling draped over a spike can provide excellent protection if the rock is sound.

protection requires some additional advice. A sound thread anchor has the advantage that it will not become unseated even if pulled in various directions, which can be very important when lead climbing—anchors can be pulled sideways or outward in a fall situation or even just due to rope drag. A sling is pushed through an opening, threaded around the back of the stopper or closure, and pushed out of the other opening. Tree trunks or roots can often be used in this way too, as long as they are strong enough. A normal webbing sling is ideal for larger threads, but often the openings are too small and require a cord sling to be used, or a thinner (and therefore weaker) webbing. This

A dead tree trunk provides temporary protection but will fail one day. Standing on the top end does not help.

A spike or thread on the lip of an overhang can prevent a nasty fall. Dave Evans on Positron (5.11b) Gogarth, North Wales.

keep the sling in place. Some spikes do not have very well-defined gaps between their back and the rock face. Examine the rock carefully, because it may be possible to ease a thinner sling into a very thin crack. Beware of very sharp edges, as they are capable of severing a rope when loaded. Slings can sometimes be encouraged to stay in place by jettisoning some larger items of protection as ballast—simply clip a few large hexes or cams to the sling. An extension sling will encourage the piece of protection to articulate rather than lift off the spike, and a variation of this theme is to tie an overhand knot in the spare webbing, especially if the top loop is weighted with spare equipment.

Most of these items are relatively easy for the second to remove, but care should be taken with threads, as simply tugging them can easily result in the material getting jammed behind the stopper. Get the knotted or sewn connection out first and then carefully ease the thread out using a nut tool to push if necessary.

can be a very awkward job to achieve one-handed while leading, and a nut extractor can therefore be useful for the leader as well as the second, making it possible to hook the loop of webbing or cord and pull it through. A piece of stiff wire with a hooked end can be more effective for this job but is less convenient to carry.

Spikes vary in shape and size from tiny protuberances through to monoliths like the Matterhorn and range similarly in shape and strength. In the same way that a coat hangs securely from a hook but tends to slip from a rounded peg, some spikes need help to

Using a nut tool to pull the end of a sling through a constricted thread.

> **TIP**
>
> Easily portable, a long 4-ft (1.2-m) sling can be used in many different ways; it can be employed to equalize anchors as well as to provide protection. Carry it doubled around the shoulders with a single twist, and with a screwgate carabiner attached to each end. When you want to use the sling, free it by unclipping the carabiner from one end.

PLACING AND REMOVING PROTECTION

Nuts and cams

Most leaders prefer to keep their wires racked in two or three bundles of similar sizes (i.e., small, medium and large) so that several can be tested in a placement if necessary before removing the carabiner holding the rest of the bundle. The choice is between carrying equipment on a bandolier (or gear sling) or gear loops on the harness. Having quickdraws on a bandolier, with nuts and cams on the harness, is probably the best combination.

A perfect nut placement is keyhole-shaped: The nut slots in at the top, wider end, and is fed by gravity into the smaller crack where it cannot fall out. For less than ideal cracks, try to get as much metal in contact with rock as possible. Get in the habit of rating placement reliability to aid your risk assessment when psyching for a move.

All wires and roped nuts can be turned sideways to fit a larger crack. This is usually much less desirable than placing a larger piece of equipment, but if you are running out of equipment, it can expand your choices.

Left: **A secure nut placement** has plenty of metal in contact with the rock and the crack tapers downward. In horizontal cracks a curved back allows a camming effect as shown here.

Below: Using a nut tool to **remove a stuck wire**.

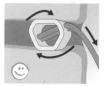

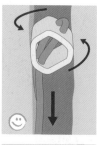

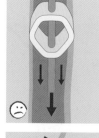

Secure hexcentric placements: Pulling the cord rotates and cams it more securely. Insecure placements: The hex is pulled downward or sideways without a camming effect.

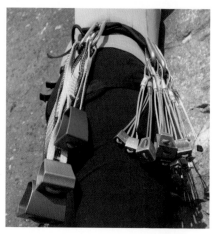

An assortment of wires and hexes: Store several sizes on one carabiner to allow an efficient choice of placements by releasing just the one carabiner.

A rack of cams: For crack climbing you may need several of the same size.

Shallow cracks, or gaps between protrusions, may only accept a sideways placement—this is better than leaving half the nut hanging in space. For harder routes carry a few tiny brass wedges (e.g., RPs) for shallow placements.

Removing nut protection
This is something of an art. Often a hard flick of an attached quickdraw upward or sideways to where the crack widens will release them. Wires that are too well seated for this method may respond to a tap with the carabiner, or may require hard prods with a nut tool—try a similar tactic for jammed hexes. Failing that, a sequence of tapping and hooking may be needed. For these really stubborn placements it may be possible to clip your harness into a higher protection point or just hang on the rope to free both hands.

Camming devices
Spring-loaded camming devices are ideal for utilizing parallel-sided cracks, and an ever-increasing range of sizes is available. Make sure your partner is equally skilled at removing them, as they are expensive and unsightly to leave behind. Most modern camming devices have flexible shafts—particularly useful for placements in horizontal cracks, as the old rigid shafts have been known to bend and eventually break when loaded if much of the shaft protrudes beyond the rock.

Camming devices hold best far outside the extremes of their range of movement. Over-cammed devices are more likely to fail when loaded but, ironically, are usually harder to remove by the second climber.

Camming devices are particularly liable to being pulled out of their intended orientation; in other words, to movement. If the device is repeatedly loaded, rotated and unloaded, it tends to creep or "walk" into or up the crack, where it may become useless if the crack widens out.

Jammed cams are particularly unsightly and costly. Resist the temptation to damage the rock, no matter how expensive the device. To remove them, both triggers need to be pulled while the shaft is simultaneously pushed, and stubborn placements might need alternate movements of the triggers. Some nut tools have a double hook that can pull both triggers if the cam is too far into the crack for fingers to reach. Sometimes a hard tap on the shaft linked to a steady pull on the triggers can persuade the cam to release.

> **TIP**
>
> If there is a choice, avoid placements that have neighboring widenings in the crack where the cam could shift to. It is a good idea to add extenders routinely to cams to reduce this tendency.

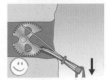

Both sides of a **camming unit** should be loaded symmetrically. In shallow pockets a flexible stem is stronger due to leverage.

ADVANCED PROTECTION TECHNIQUES

Micro-wires will hold little more than body weight but may help steady the nerves while seeking more substantial placements. On harder leads, several tiny wire placements may be the only available equipment—perhaps equalized with a sling to share the loading. Arranging a cluster of protection points is a good policy in any case before committing to a sequence. If one is displaced as you move away, this gives backup protection.

Moving past a piece of protection can pull it sideways or outward, unseating the placement if this has not been anticipated. This can often be avoided by linking the equipment to another placement designed simply to counteract the pull. A good example is linking a sling over a spike to another sling around a downward-pointing spike, in order to prevent the piece of protection from lifting off. Wires and sometimes cams placed in horizontal breaks will often only work if pulled in one direction. An opposing nut can be linked to it, holding the equipment in place for its optimal loading.

This peg could not be lassoed from below as the eye touches the rock. Instead it has been **girth-hitched** to reduce leverage.

The vector forces involved in traverses are an often neglected aspect of lead climbing. If a climb meanders, a fall will tug the pieces of protection sideways (unless they have all been extended sufficiently so that the rope runs straight, like on a thoughtfully bolted sport

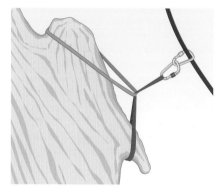

Two virtually useless spikes have been combined by tensioning a sling, to create **excellent protection**.

A **micro-wire** in a tiny crack. The cracks on all sides of this placement mean that it would probably rip out in the event of a fall.

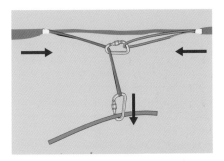

Opposing nuts in horizontal and vertical cracks help load the nut toward the crack constriction rather than allowing rope drag or a fall to rotate a single piece toward a wider opening.

climb). The resulting force bisects the angle that the rope passes through the protection point, so the placement could be pulled up and out. It has been known for all the lower pieces of protection to be ripped out by a falling climber because of vector pulls. If the top protection point then fails, this can be disastrous. Make good use of extenders, and reinforce crucial protection points so they can cope with different angles of pull. An important protection point at the start of a traverse can be reinforced with another point designed to oppose the upward pull. Link them together as you would equalize a belay.

Psychological placements

A psychological placement is a weak or poor piece of protection that is unlikely to hold a real fall. Of course, a trusted placement is always the preferred choice. Psychological placements should be used only with double-ropes, where the other rope is clipped into the nearest good placement. Often just a body-weight psychological placement is enough to help you get your mind together and stop shaking. If nothing else, it may be enough to descend from if you still can't get it together. There are several options:

- **Thin slings:** Carry two types: thin cord—$1/8$ in (3–4 mm) diameter, maybe with a hexcentric attached for added versatility— and thin tape, no more than $2/5$ in (10 mm) wide. Spectra tapes are excellent for easing behind a spike with minimal clearance.

- **Threading sling:** This is just a thin sling with a piece of stiff wire attached—invaluable for small threads.
- **Skyhook:** Quick to place in extremis and often relatively stable. For marginal placements, linking to a downward-pointing spike or wire may give an excellent protection point. Another tactic is to pull lots of rope through on one of your ropes and tie it to the hook. The second stands on this rope to hold it in place. The other rope is clipped in as protection. Once the move is completed and the equipment obtained, the hook can be flicked off and popped back into your chalk bag, a good place to store it.
- **Extender:** For poor pegs, a clove-hitched longer extender around the stem reduces leverage. If the peg is difficult to reach, a slipknot can be flicked over the eye and pulled tight.

TIP

Practice lassoing spikes and pegs with a long sling, or even two connected together.

A skyhook protection point held in place with a sling tied to a poor wire creates an anchor that won't lift off of its tiny ledge.

ROPE HANDLING AND ROPE SYSTEMS

All rope systems require some care to prevent the rope from tangling. Starting with a pile of coiled rope, uncoil a length at each end so one end of the rope is sticking out from the bottom of the pile, and the other is sticking out from the top. The leader should tie on to the top end. On multi-pitch climbs, the leader's end of the rope(s) should be at the top of the pile, so this is an advantage of leading through; i.e., the second on the pitch below arrives at the stance and takes over the lead. If the same person is leading all pitches, all rope will need to be "flaked," i.e., passed through the hands to reverse the order of the coils. If this is not done a tangle is virtually guaranteed.

There are three types of rope systems for normal climbing. These are the single-rope, twin-rope and half-rope (usually known, confusingly, as double-rope) systems. Choosing an appropriate system depends mainly on the type of climbing you plan to do.

Single rope
Ideal for top-roping and leading single-pitch sport climbs, this is also useful for novice trad climbers on straightforward pitches. The rope is normally around 2/5 in (10–11 mm) in diameter.
Pros: Simple rope handling; hard-wearing; lighter; less prone to tangling.
Cons: Long fall potential when clipping a protection point; difficult to retreat

from long climbs; hard to protect traverses; high potential for rope drag and pieces of protection rotating outward; no backup if the rope is cut; relatively high impact forces sustained by the climber and top anchor.

Twin rope
This is the lightest system for multi-pitch routes and is ideal for long bolted routes. Two ropes are clipped into every protection point and are treated by the belayer as if they are a single rope. The ropes are usually about 3/10 in (7–8 mm) in diameter.
Pros: Full-rope length rappels; very light; fairly simple rope handling; backup if one is cut in an accident.
Cons: Ropes should not be used individually; also, most

Single-rope system: The single rope is clipped to all protection points in this simple system.

Twin-rope system: Both ropes clipped to all protection points but allow a full-length retrievable rappel.

Double-rope system with half-ropes: Individual ropes are clipped to most effective protection.

86

Double ropes used to minimize friction and protect the leader when clipping a new placement.

of the potential problems associated with a single rope.

Half ("double") rope

A compromise two-rope system particularly suited to complex lines and less certain protection. The ropes are often clipped into alternate protection points to reduce the likely fall distance if one point fails—particularly if the leader can see that the high placement is relatively poor—or if a fall is taken while pulling the rope up to make a clip. Alternatively the ropes can follow parallel lines and make best use of strategic protection points to protect traverses. The system works best with ropes of contrasting colors; they are normally $1/3$ in (8–9 mm) in diameter.

Pros: Less prone to rope drag; full-length rappels possible; easier to rig multiple anchors; backup if a protection point or rope fails for any reason.

Cons: Prone to tangling; difficult rope handling for the belayer; confusing if both are the same color.

Double-rope technique: Handling double ropes

Belaying with double ropes requires some practice. One rope is cupped between the lower fingers, while the rope to be paid out or drawn in is trapped between the thumb and index finger. If the leader falls, the belayer squeezes both ropes in the belay hand. Attentive belaying can help the leader enormously.

Suppose the leader is using blue and red ropes. The second pays out blue rope as the leader pulls it to clip into a protection point far above the leader's head. When the leader commits to the sequence, the red rope must be paid out as the blue rope is taken in until the leader's waist passes the protection point—after that both ropes should be paid out together.

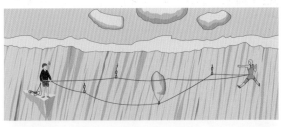

Double ropes used effectively on a traverse to minimize potential swings if the second climber falls off.

> **TIP**
>
> Clear instructions should be called out by the leader when double-roping.

PROTECTING THE SECOND CLIMBER

For a team ascent of a route it is important that the lead climber considers the climber(s) who will be following the pitch. For a team of three this is relatively straightforward for the middle climber, who can follow the pitch belayed by both the leader and third climber, giving protection from both directions if the trail rope is clipped into protection points as they are passed. This minimizes the distance the second climber can swing even on a poorly protected traverse. The final climber, however, has to remove pieces of protection and can face a large pendulum if a slip occurs immediately after unfastening a protection point. Some forethought can reduce and sometimes eliminate this problem. One way is simply to place plenty of protection along the traverse so there is never far to swing in the event of a fall.

On wandering routes the leader can often place protection after a tricky move, in a position that keeps the rope suspended directly above the difficulties. A considerate leader will try not to place protection midway through a sequence, as this will force the final climber to hang in a difficult position to remove them. Sometimes it is possible for the leader to place "temporary" protection points to protect the move, complete the sequence, and place a good protection point from a resting place, then reach or even climb down to remove the temporary equipment.

Tall climbers should be wary of placing protection at full reach out to the sides of the climbing line as this may force a shorter partner into precarious contortions in order to retrieve the equipment, often creating a difficult move that would otherwise be avoidable.

The author leading A Dream of White Horses (HVS, 4c), a classic traverse in North Wales. **Careful thought** is required to protect the second climber on difficult moves.

Double ropes and back ropes

Double-rope technique can be used particularly effectively to protect traverses for both the leader and the second. One rope may protect moves before and perhaps along the traverse, while the other protects the far end. If it is not possible to place equipment on the actual traverse, protection placed high above the midway point might be found, minimizing the pendulum potential for the second when following the pitch.

For tricky moves on a traverse where the second will face a pendulum, a back rope may make an enormous difference. This involves leaving a carabiner on a protection point just before the move and clipping one rope into it. The belayer takes in on one rope and pays out on the other as the climber traverses. At the end of the traverse the climber unties from this back rope and pulls it all from the carabiner. This should only be undertaken by experienced climbers as it has the potential for serious errors to be made, especially if conditions make communication difficult.

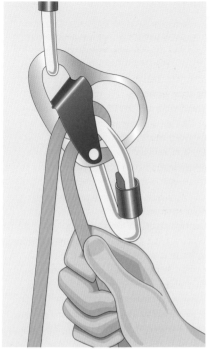

Using a Reverso—a typical self-locking device for bringing up one or two partners. However, this device is awkward for paying out rope if a climber needs to reverse a move.

> **TIP**
>
> Communication makes an enormous difference, so try to belay where you can see the second for as much of the pitch as possible. This may mean extending the connection to the anchors, but the extra work usually pays off, especially if teamed with less experienced climbers.

This climber has left the red rope running through a carabiner that he was willing to abandon in order to **protect a difficult move** near the start of a traverse. The result is that a fall now should not result in a big swing across the cliff if he falls off on the way over to the next protection point (clipped to the blue rope).

BODY POSITION AND BALANCE

Using the body effectively

The body is a series of levers with muscles to move them. The core or trunk of your body is where all the levers attach, and where the majority of your weight resides. It is the center of your body by weight.

Climbing can be regarded as a flowing series of movements by the body's trunk. For most adult males this core is about 1 in (2.5 cm) above the navel and is slightly lower in women, but the exact location is affected by the weight of the legs compared to the upper body and so is unique to every individual. Awareness of the relationship between the core and the points of contact will pay off enormously in allowing you to climb efficiently, as the body needs to start and finish each sequence in a state of balance. Most climbing movements require the levers to rotate, with your weight moving back and forth from hold to hold.

Your center of gravity has to be balanced between whatever contact you have with the rock and the ubiquitous force of gravity.

> **TIP**
>
> Effective use of the body often demands harmony between the left and the right sides. Often the right hand works in partnership with the left foot, and vice versa.

Balance exercises

Stand with your feet braced at shoulder-width, so your core is comfortably midway between your legs. Without shifting your point of balance it is not possible to lift either foot, and on the rock face trying to do this would waste arm strength from fighting gravity. If you are leaning right to reach a hold, your weight will be concentrated on the right foot. So to initiate a step left it is often more efficient to lean right first in order to free the foot to move.

Find somewhere with a selection of sideholds. Where do you need to get your body weight in relation to a sidehold to get it to work? Move up, using a sidehold. How does the weight shift? Move up, down and sideways off sideholds, and continue to think

Above: Using his **center of gravity**, this climber can keep his feet vertically jammed against the ridge, freeing up his right hand to place protection.

Left: Knut Burgdorf leading Korallenpfeiler (5.11c), a tricky sandstone pillar in Berdorf, Luxemburg. Precise **footwork and excellent balance** are imperative when climbing with such small pinches.

Good footwork is clearly allowing this climber to use her hands only for balance.

A supple pelvis allows this climber to keep his weight close to the rock and directly over his feet.

about the relationship to your body weight. Try the same exercise with downward-pointing holds; these are known as underclings. Keep your body weight close in to the rock and then lean out. Which feels more strenuous? Which allows you to step up more easily?

Find somewhere with slabs and climb with clenched fists. If this is not practical, try climbing with your hands at waist level, or only using your thumbs. Find an easy angled slab and try to climb it without using your hands at all. Repeat it a few times while concentrating on those balance shifts. Notice how your weight needs to stay over the foothold until a critical moment when the

other foot is ready to accept your weight. Try it with your eyes shut, doing it by feel; learn to listen to the messages your body sends you.

Experiment with actively shifting your center of gravity on overhanging rock. While your center of gravity is directly above your feet, they can be taking all the weight. The further your torso is pushed outward, the harder your arms will have to pull to keep you on the rock. The upper body can be brought inward by adopting a "frogs' legs" posture or by turning your pelvis and pulling it in toward the rock. Try traversing a wall using only the outside edge of one foot and the inside of the other and notice how your pelvis becomes oriented at right angles to the wall. Climbing an overhanging wall on jug holds can allow you to experiment by swinging your pelvis to face the opposite direction with each move.

Side pulls can be used most effectively when performed in opposition to the center of gravity. Here the climber's weight is to the right of the vertical edge.

> ### TIP
> Practice moving your feet up and using your thigh muscles to move your torso up. Climbers who stretch too much are often not making effective use of intermediate footholds, and can find the feet popping off the holds on slab climbs, reinforcing a lack of trust.

USING THE FEET EFFECTIVELY

Good footwork is so fundamental to climbing that a well-fitting pair of quality climbing shoes should be any climber's first acquisition; otherwise a mistrust of small edges and pockets will become ingrained. As footwork improves, stamina and power will also seem to improve due to the exponential increase in efficiency.

Practice on a variety of rock types to increase versatility. Climbing walls, for example, tend to lack slab-like footholds and cracks. Making a transition from granite to limestone or vice versa can be baffling at first; it can seem like there are hardly any footholds until the appropriate style of edging or smearing is developed.

Footwork exercises

Bouldering with pebbles balanced loosely on the backs of the hands (you can rest fingertips on the rock for balance) or with clenched fists can help build confidence in the feet.

Encourage accuracy and precision in foot placements by climbing in slow motion or with silent steps. This is especially effective on indoor climbing walls where the hollow boards echo.

> **TIP**
>
> Footwork exercises can be enhanced by a "first-attempt" rule, so that once a toe has made contact with a hold it cannot be replaced on the same hold. This means the heels can be rotated but the toe has to be carefully placed.

This climber is using the **outside edge of the shoe**, but bringing the heel out a little may allow the toe to be used more effectively.

Tackle a boulder or climbing wall with plenty of holds. Count the number of foot placements you use: try for the maximum and then the minimum number of steps. Which style demanded the most energy? Which involved more dramatic shifts of balance? Stepping high and throwing your weight onto the upper foot is known as a rock-on, a strenuous maneuver that can often be avoided by the ability to spot and use small footholds. Keep experimenting with footholds, paper-thin edges and changes in angle; all will take some weight off your arms.

Edging

Keep the sole of your foot flat and rigid and focus the front area of the shoe onto holds. Novices tend to use the mid-sole, which gives less "feel" and seriously restricts your reach. When using the outside edges, imagine you are curling your toes over each foothold.

On a climbing wall with textured panels, traversing increasingly steep walls without using bolt-on holds can increase your awareness of what the feet can stick to.

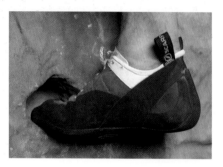

This climber has inserted a toe in a hole in the rock, known as **a pocket**. Shaped toes allow small pockets to be used.

Using the big toe (inside edge) effectively.

Smearing

Explore the limits of friction by walking up, down and across progressively harder sections of a low slab until your feet slip. The angle of rock they can tolerate depends on a combination of the rock type and also your belief. Friction climbing is perhaps the most Zen-like of all climbing styles. The goal is to get as much rubber as possible in contact with the rock. On easy-angled slabs the entire front foot can be used, but on steeper rock the edges must be smeared.

The front end of the whole shoe is used for **smearing** here. Any surface can be used.

You don't have to be this supple to use a **heel hook** but note how the body hangs from the foot as if it were an extra hand.

Positive reinforcement from successful feedback will help enormously to stay calm on run-out slabs.

Hooking

Practice using your heel like a prehensile limb, pulling the body toward a hold. This technique requires well-fitting heels, otherwise the heel can pop out of the shoe—climbing in slippers does not suit this style of movement. Try using heel hooks to cross large overhangs, using body torsion to pull the body into the rock between hand shifts. Camming the heel against a flake and the toe against the wall is often a very effective variation.

HANDHOLDS

Types
Every hold is different, but there are five basic ways to use them depending on their size, position and shape.

The open-hand grip
This is the classic hand shape, used for large and rounded holds ("slopers"). With flat and incut holds this grip can allow long reaches to be made and is not very demanding on tendons. For smaller and rounded holds or pockets this grip can be tiring and very reliant on the texture of the rock. The thumb may be able to push inward on the side of the hold, or even used as the only digit in a shallow scoop.

The reverse open-hand grip (palming hold)
Pushing downward on a slab or bulge with the palm of the hand can allow the extension muscles to be used if the angle is low enough to allow good friction.

Using a large *incut hold*, often called a "jug" or "bucket." This open grip also works for flat-topped holds.

The climber is **palming** a slab (left) and a bulge (right), requiring only friction. Palming can conserve energy as no muscular effort is required to use the hold.

CHALK
Most climbers use gymnast's chalk to improve their grip. Try to minimize your reliance on chalk by only using it when really necessary. Dipping the hand can become a nervous habit and waste energy on strenuous climbs.

 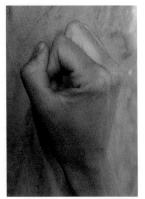

A crimp hold: Note the reverse curve of the first two joints of the fingers (far left), and using the thumb hooked over the fingers (left) to help hang onto a tiny crimp.

Pinching a fluting: Squeeze the rock between the fingers and the thumb.

The crimp grip
The hand is bunched and the last joint of the fingers flexed inward to utilize smaller finger holds. Sometimes the thumb is placed over the index finger to gain extra strength. This demands tendon strength and can lead to injuries if overused. Crimps are most effective when pulling straight down, so long reaches are very strenuous as the elbow becomes forced outward.

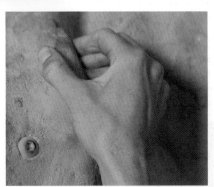

The pinch grip
Holds that protrude from the surface, fins of rock, limestone tufa and the side of cracks can be used by pinching the rock between the thumb and fingers. Some pinches are horizontally oriented and might be used with the thumb down if high or with the thumb above and fingers below to allow a long reach from a low hold.

The jam
Jamming is a versatile technique used mainly for crack climbing, but can also be applied to pockets and slots. A solid jam can be very energy-efficient as the tendons can relax.

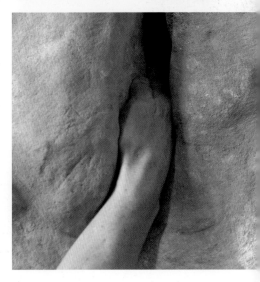

A secure hand jam: The thumb is pulled down behind cupped fingers to lock securely.

HANDHOLDS

Orientation

Holds can face in any direction. Novice climbers often only spot the horizontal breaks, but these are not always the best solution to a sequence.

Sideways holds

Vertical or diagonal holds give side pulls. These run more or less parallel to the direction of gravity, so to use them the center of gravity must be kept out to the side. If combined with careful footwork and balance, the body can pivot from the hold and height can be gained even on overhanging rock. Side pulls can also be very useful for initiating a long reach diagonally or sideways in the opposite direction, since the arm and wrist can be fully straightened.

Sideholds are often used in opposition, i.e., opposing directions on either side of the body. Careful body position and core tension

The late, great Todd Skinner using the "elevator door" **double Gaston** to good effect on the Great Canadian Knife (VI, 5.13b), Mount Proboscis.

Using a tight finger crack, this climber counteracts gravity by stemming his foot against the corner.

TIP

Sometimes sideholds can be found in the side walls of a wide crack, allowing the climber to make easy progress without resorting to off-width techniques, by leaning the shoulders straight out from the rock face. It is always a sensible option to check the depths of a crack for side pulls.

STRATEGIES FOR MAKING THE BEST USE OF HOLDS

- The same hold might be used as a crimp when first reached at arm's length, then turned into a pinch or sidehold as the body moves past it, before being used finally as a foothold.
- By varying the way a hold is used and by using different types of holds, you can modify the muscle groups used and therefore conserve energy. An undercut or side pull following a strenuous sequence of crimps can release lactic acid buildup and allow at least partial recovery.
- Chalk should be used sparingly: It is best saved as a "secret weapon" for crux moves on small or sloping holds. Climbers often waste valuable energy chalking up when it is not necessary.
- On smaller fingerholds the fingers are more powerful if pressed together—if there is not room for all the fingers the muscle/tendon system is optimized by curling the remaining fingers up.

is needed to move between opposing holds, in order to counteract the "barn-door effect" of the body rotating outward around a side hold, like a door opening on a hinge.

The Gaston is a strenuous method of using side pulls, named after the famous French climber Gaston Rebuffat. The technique is used when it is not possible to get the center of gravity out to the side. The elbow is bent so the hand is near the shoulder—the thumb pointing downward. When used with both hands pulling on either side of the crack, this technique is like trying to pull elevator doors open.

Downward holds

Some rock features point downward and may provide underclings (undercuts). These can be very useful as the wrist can be straightened, allowing a very long reach upward. In particular they occur under overhangs where their use is often crucial to enable the climber to reach over the lip of the "roof." Underclings feel tenuous if first reached above the head, but as the feet are moved higher and the body raises, they feel increasingly positive. Undercling flakes have a tendency to be loose or hollow, so they should be tested before relying on them fully.

Pockets

Holes in the rock can vary from tiny air pockets to enormous caves. Finger pockets are particularly common in limestone and may require a great deal of finger strength to use effectively; the middle and ring finger combination is the strongest for small holds. Monos will only accept one finger, demanding accurate footwork to avoid injuries. Some pockets have hidden sideholds within them, or the edges can be used to provide side pulls or underclings. Sometimes the thumb can be inserted in the lip to undercling a small high pocket, and then swapped for fingers as the waist moves above the pocket.

> **TIP**
>
> Bouldering with your eyes closed, with or without a partner giving instructions, will increase your concentration on other feedback, especially touch and the location of your body's center of gravity. Your partner could even describe the handholds and footholds and specify how to use them.

Using an undercling effectively: A positive undercling hold may allow the climber to relax with a straight arm. Straightening the legs allows the climber to make a long reach upward; in fact a reach of more than 12 in (30 cm) higher is possible from the pictured undercling.

97

LAYBACKING AND STEMMING

These are useful techniques that, although associated in particular with "open-book" corners, can be modified for use almost anywhere.

Laybacking

Laybacking is a strenuous technique that opposes the body's center of gravity against side pulls. The overall feeling is that only the hands are preventing the shoulders from falling backward. It is mainly used in corners and on arêtes, but layaway moves can also be found on walls, particularly when using flakes. Laybacking relies on a combination of good technique, strength and determination: a keen awareness of your center of gravity is required in order to prevent your body barn-dooring outward, and often the hips and shoulders are touching the rock in order to work against gravity. Laybacking an arête can be particularly difficult as handholds may be rounded and footholds smeared, while the barn-door tendency is more pronounced. Sometimes heel hooks are required to lock the center of gravity in order to move a hand up.

Laybacking is more efficient if the hands and feet can be kept lower: as the feet are forced higher on steeper laybacks with featureless walls, holding the opposition effect becomes increasingly strenuous. Similarly, long reaches between side pulls require one hand to be locked-off in order to make the reach and this can be extremely hard work. Look for footholds directly below the shoulders that may release some of the weight from the hands. The arms are best kept straight to prevent them from becoming pumped and the inside hand is usually kept highest. The hands

Above: **Laybacking a blunt arête** requires excellent balance to prevent the body from pivoting outward like a barn door.

Left: **Laybacking a crack** like this is strenuous and also requires body awareness. Look for jams to rest.

Stemming allows this corner to be easily climbed despite poor holds. Outward pressure allows smears to be used by hands and feet.

A crucifix move in a corner. Pressing down with the hands allows both feet to be moved simultaneously.

and feet can be shuffled or leapfrogged up the rock, but generally crossing over either the hands or the feet will tend to put more weight onto the arms. Jamming the ball of a foot allows a camming effect that helps to counteract the swinging effect and recruits different thigh muscles.

Stemming

The name of this technique describes its classic form where the feet are placed on facing walls of a corner with the body's weight distributed evenly. Like an arch, the body's weight pushes the feet into the holds, allowing smears and ripples to be used if necessary. Stemming with the feet near the outside edges of an overhanging corner can allow the body to remain upright and this can often allow the arms to recover even on exceptionally steep and intimidating terrain.

Stemming can also be used on widely spaced footholds on the same wall. Parallel cracks or ribs

can be used, and the outward pressure allows even vertical edges to be used if the legs are spread widely.

Crucifix move

This is a strenuous stemming move using the arms instead of the legs. The upper body is locked by applying outward pressure on the hands at anything up to shoulder level, allowing the feet to be brought over a bulge or blank section. Crucifix moves are often used in conjunction with standard stemming to tackle wide chimneys.

TIP

A useful exercise to gain confidence in stemming is to climb a corner using the feet only—this requires dynamic weight transfer onto a foot in order to jump the other one up to the next hold. Another good practice exercise is climbing a corner using smears only.

FINGER AND HAND CRACK CLIMBING

Crack climbing comes as a relatively alien technique, particularly for people who learn to climb on an indoor wall, so practice on a top-rope first. Some cracks are best tackled by laybacking, even if the side wall is only wide enough for toes. Other cracks might be climbed entirely by jamming fingers, hands and toes into the crack, perhaps interspersed with the occasional layback move.

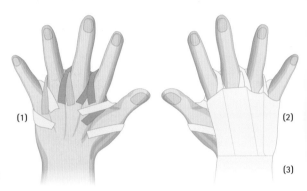

(1)   (2)

(3)

Taping hands for crack climbing: (1) Wrap thin strips around fingers and thumb. This can be sticky side up. (2) Stick wider strips onto the thin strips to cover the back of the hand. (3) Wrap a strip around the wrist to keep this "glove" in place.

Taping up

Jamming is painful even at the best of times. Poor technique results in grazes,

Use **finger jams** in a tapering crack like a good nut placement. Thin tape around the finger knuckles can help.

but rock crystals will dig into the flesh of even the best crack climbers. Zinc oxide tape can be simply wrapped around the knuckles to provide protection for finger jamming, or used to improvise gloves with bare palms. The tape is strapped around the fingers first and

> **TIP**
>
> For cracks that are wider than the knuckles, try inserting the fingers in the crack and the thumb downward against the wall. Another technical jam is a thumb placed in the crack and wedged in place using a finger.

then onto the back of the hand. If removed with care, these are reusable.

Finger jamming

The fingers are inserted into a crack, ideally above a constriction that allows the knuckles to jam. For smooth cracks with parallel sides, twisting the hand is necessary to torque the fingers. The top hand is normally best inserted in the "thumbs down" position while the lower hand can have the thumbs up or down. Placing the thumb downward puts leverage and torque into the jam, which increases as the body moves higher. The "thumb upward" method of jamming will allow a longer reach to be made for the next placement.

Some constrictions can be utilized best by cupping

Using a thumb "sprag"—push the side wall with the thumb to increase torque.

For short openings that are wider than a finger, it may be necessary to cross fingers to obtain a jam.

Experiment with bending the little finger to help lock the ring finger.

the thumb and finger around them like an "OK" sign.

Hand jamming

When the crack allows the hand to slide in as far as the wrist, hand jams can be used. Don't reach too far above your head or you will tire quickly. Push the fingers against one side of the crack and the hand will jam. As the crack widens, place the thumb into the palm of the hand, giving it more bulk. When it gets too wide, form your hand into a cupped or full-fist shape, turn it sideways, and jam the fleshy sides of the thumb and pinkie.

Foot and toe jams

The basic foot jam is best learned in a hand crack. Slot your foot (big toe up, little toe down) into the crack up to the arch of your foot, with your knee out to the side, then torque your knee toward the crack to

twist the shoe into place and raise your waist ready to move the hands to higher jams. Bring your hips in close to the wall at the end of each movement, in order to transfer weight off your arms and onto your feet. Your ankles should feel like they're holding most of your weight, and your hands are simply holding you in place while you step up.

With straightforward jams it should feel like you are almost walking up the crack.

For narrower cracks only the toes or tips can be inserted into the cracks. Lift the knees even higher, so that the little toes are inserted more sideways, and then stretch your legs, frog-like, to move up the crack. Keep the finger jams fairly low with this technique.

Indian Creek, Moab, Utah, is regarded as one of the world's greatest destinations for developing crack climbing technique. This climber is fully committed to hand and foot jams in a crack that breaches a smooth wall, offering no faceholds.

CHIMNEYS AND OFF-WIDTHS

Chimneys

Chimneys are slots that are big enough to get your whole body into: the widest chimneys may only be spanned by launching across the void to land with the fingertips on one side and the feet on the other.

To have any success at climbing chimneys you would do well to watch a caterpillar in action. Alternate sets of muscles are locked off to allow the body to bend and bring up the lower legs, or extend and send out the upper limbs. Lock your body across the crack, using footholds on one wall and your backside on the other. If there are plenty of footholds on the wall, you can simply move a foot up, then wriggle your torso up by using each shoulder blade in turn, like little hands. One shoulder pushes against the wall while the other is hunched up high, then the weight is transferred to this upper shoulder. After a few of these wriggles, the backside can be released by locking your shoulders against the wall. Arch your back, replace your backside on the wall a few inches higher, and start wriggling again.

Chimneys often don't provide much in the way of footholds. Check both walls before committing to facing a particular direction, and be prepared to rotate at various points in the cleft to make the best use of the available holds. If there are no footholds in a wide chimney, bring your knees level with your chest so your heels can touch the rock. An important variation is to use your lower legs in a scissor action, one on each wall. The feet should be high, so the heel of one foot will probably touch your backside. By pushing outward, the legs can be straightened, allowing the upper body to be released, then quickly moved up and locked again.

Back and footing in a narrow corridor. This is at the maximum span for this technique but notice how each foot is flat against a wall. In narrower chimneys it may be the knee that presses against the far wall.

Spanning a wide chimney at Arapiles (Djurid), Australia.

Using the arms to assist progress is an important aspect of chimneying. Very often the most effective technique is to place your palms on the rock, level with your backside. Scoops and hollows allow your hands to be used in opposition to your feet, allowing both shoulders to be moved up without having to wriggle them individually.

Chimneying is very strenuous, so finding resting opportunities is essential. Utilizing straight limbs rather than opposing muscle groups is the key, so footholds help

Using arm bars and leverage on the crack edge to climb a narrow chimney.

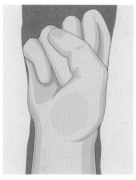

A fist jam: These sideways placements feel insecure at first.

Stacked jams: These are used to tackle a wider crack.

> **TIP**
>
> Beware of using knee jams like knuckles, as they are prone to getting stuck.

a lot. You may also be able to rotate your pelvis and stem the gap with a foot on each side, thus releasing the upper body completely. In tighter chimneys, resting is more challenging, but some recovery is often possible using a knee bar. With a heel tucked under your backside, lift the knee and place it on the opposite wall, then ease down so that the bone locks diagonally across the cleft. This allows you to span the gap with no muscular exertion.

Off-widths

These are cracks wider than fist-width but too narrow for chimneying. A good off-width style is fluid and continuous, like swimming. The aim is to use the arms

This climber is wriggling up an **off-width crack**. The lower body has been wedged allowing the arms to be moved up again.

and legs to apply pressure to opposite sides of the crack. Push an arm in until just beyond the shoulder, then bend the elbow to press the palm against one side and the elbow and shoulder against the other. If the elbow is lifted higher an arm-bar lock may allow some rest. Meanwhile the outside arm pulls on the edge of the crack at neck level. Some off-widths are notoriously difficult to jam. Sometimes the only way is to stack the hands side by side as fist-to-hand or even double-fists.

The legs can be jammed by locking a foot against one wall and the knee against the other or, for narrower slots, by jamming your heel and toe in the crack. If the crack is just too wide for heel/toe jamming, try stacking them in a "T" shape.

Speed and efficiency are of the essence on overhanging rock because gravity has the advantage. Regular practice pays off enormously here. This is partly because you'll be fitter, but more importantly because you'll be able to work out solutions more efficiently. At a conceptual level, you'll be able to remember a successful solution to something relatively similar. At a physical level, the message from your brain will work on the opposing muscle groups much more effectively when following recently used pathways (often termed "engrams").

Weight taken by your feet is released from your arms. The most fundamental technique is to rotate your pelvis so that one hip faces away from the rock. Normally this will involve using the big toe of one foot and the little toe of the other (in other words, the inside and outside edges of your shoes). This enables you to bring your pelvis in toward the rock so your weight is taken more by your feet. It also allows you to utilize sideholds for your feet with Egyptian moves (see page 111).

Having transferred some more weight onto your feet, capitalize by using twist locks across your body. Point your chest in the same

Continuously overhanging rock is best tackled efficiently to hold enough strength to tackle the final moves.

> **TIP**
>
> It's often worth a little chalk dab to signpost small footholds, as they often become harder to see as you move up and are trying to look back under the bulge.

Using body torque, this climber has locked her arm across her chest to make a long reach with the other hand.

A **toe hooked under a flake** (below) allows this climber to pull his lower body closer to the rock, while the author uses a **heel hook** (right) to take weight off his arms on Night Glue (5.13b) in Pen Trwyn, North Wales.

direction as your pelvis, and the arm on that side will be locked, with the other shoulder higher and thus closer to the next hold. It is often also possible to face straight into the rock, lock off hard and then snatch upward. However, this requires a lot more power as your torso will want to rotate outward as you release one hand.

Another key skill for tackling overhanging rock is using your feet creatively. Try to actively pull your pelvis in toward the rock by daggering your foot into the rock. Sometimes a foot can prevent the body from swinging out by hooking under a projection facing away from the direction of travel. Heel hooks are often particularly effective on steep rock; a heel on a hold out on the lip of an overhang is like a third hand and can allow one arm to be released. Sometimes it may be possible to prevent swings by "hugging" pillars with the feet. Flagging with one of the feet to act as a counterbalance is often also helpful if there aren't good footholds where you want them.

Rests

The best places to rest are usually before and after the overhang, but with more sustained sequences, some recovery is going to be required. Heel hooks and similar foot maneuvers are

helpful, and sometimes it is possible to throw a knee lock that allows you to release both hands. This is either a foothold conveniently placed to allow your knee to crush up against the roof or a sideways lock with the lower limb spanning a wide crack, or between two tufas, etc.

Partial recovery can be made by changing between holds—each hold uses different tensions. Side pulls and hand jams are better than flat holds for allowing the body to be held in to the rock. Try to release one hand in order to shake out the lactic acid and to chalk up. When you are ready to move on, start from a straight-arm position, pull up with both hands, then continue the momentum by making the reach.

A good **knee lock** allows this climber to recover with a no-hands rest.

CLIMBING SLABS

The first principle of slab climbing is to get your weight into your feet. *Really* into your feet. This is where all that practice testing the limits of adherence at your local bouldering venue pays off. Often on slab climbs, you are not looking for a projecting foothold, but dimples or subtle changes in gradient. Don't bother with that lichenous hold—nobody else has used it or it would be clean. And if you try to use it your foot will skid on the lichen.

Pure slab climbing demands total reliance on friction, so practicing in less than ideal conditions can be counterproductive, as your mind may learn to mistrust sensory impressions from your feet. On a dry day, you can climb easy-angled slabs by simply padding up them, hands open wide and simply pushing away from the rock so that all your weight is thrust onto your feet.

As you move onto steeper or smoother rock, toeholds become necessary. Again, faith is often the key. Place a toe onto a change in angle, with the other toes lower. Grind the toe into the rock as you pivot the other toes upward; once the rubber has bitten it will stay put and absorb all your weight. This is sometimes known as "worm grinding"—an effective metaphor. The trick is to get your weight completely onto the foot in one flowing movement, then place the other foot, ease just enough pressure into it to start biting, and shift your balance onto it. Usually your feet only slip when they are not fully weighted, so try to make your weight transfer smooth and continuous.

Small handholds can often be utilized on slab climbs if combined with good footwork. Often you will want to use the hold from full-arm stretch above your head through to pushing fully down. Stretching exercises will help if you want to step up onto the same hold. For really finger-reliant stuff, hooking your thumb over the fingertips will often help by sharing the load. For low, rounded holds, often the palm of your hand with fingers pointing downward is really effective, and there are times when the thumb alone, stuffed downward into a dimple, is more effective than fingers. Don't overlook side pulls, both for your fingers and your feet. If necessary, rotate your knee inward so that your heel is raised and your toes point downward as they push out onto the sidehold.

The best way to improve your slab climbing is to team up with somebody who is better at it, and get them to lead. There will come a time when you say to yourself, "I could have led that quicker and better myself"; it will feel very different when you come to take over the sharp end, but with the mileage under your belt, at least you will know that you have the potential to spot the holds.

Typical **slab climbing** in Eldorado, Switzerland. The climber relies almost entirely on friction for footholds.

Slab climbing often demands **long run-outs** between protection points. Even where cracks exist they are often too shallow to accept protection.

DYNAMIC MOVES, ROCK-ONS AND MANTELING

The moves described below all require an element of timing, as the body weight is transferred upward or sideways dynamically.

Dynamic moves
Slaps and udges
These involve a fast movement of the hand from one hold to another. This can be the most efficient way of transferring holds but can also be effective when you find yourself unable to make a static reach. The "slap" requires determination and timing to be effective. Focus attention on the hold and if possible take a look at the texture of the part you are planning to grab, then commit to the move. It is easier to slap for a hold that has the same orientation as the one that you are launching from, and also if the rest of the body can remain still. Simple one-handed traversing on a wall is excellent training for this kind of movement.

The "udge" starts as a static reach for a hold, but the last few inches are just beyond the comfortable point of balance and require a sudden committing acceleration to reach the hold. Sometimes an intermediate sloping hold can be used momentarily to gather resources for the final surge.

Dynos
These are the climber's leap of faith, launching from a "spring" body position and ending in a "catch." A good spring preparation puts the feet in the best position to support the body at the end of the dyno.

A full dyno involves most or all of the limbs becoming airborne, and the body describes a "C" pattern in the air. Start with your feet relatively high and spaced

A full dyno: This committing move shows the climber in midair, with only a hooked heel as contact.

comfortably, with your body close to the rock. Push aggressively with your feet, levering out on straight arms, but as your arms pass horizontal, pull so that your momentum is directed up and inward to the hold. Try to grab the hold just before the still point where upward motion has ceased but the descent has not begun (the dead point) and focus on getting your feet back and stabilizing the body position.

In a double dyno both hands launch out simultaneously for a high break: This feels more committing, as a fall is the inevitable result of failure.

> **TIP**
>
> Dynos should only be performed when you have warmed up, and a climbing gym with safe landings is an excellent place to practice. As confidence grows, try diagonal dynos and overhanging dynos as well.

This climber has made a fast slap from a hold to the sharp edge. Note how the rest of the body does not move.

Completing a rock-on: This climber is moving her center of gravity upward and left over a foothold that started out to the side.

Manteling onto a single hold: The climber pushes up to lock the arms straight, then prepares to ease a foot onto the same hold.

Rock-ons

A toe or heel on a hold at about waist height is used to pull the body weight up and over. These moves can be very strenuous if attempted statically so they are generally best treated as a dynamic move, launching from a good foothold and "throwing" the hips by using side pulls or pushing down on a hold behind the hips. Rock-ons are often the key to difficult slab moves.

Manteling

A high ledge is grasped at arm's reach and then the feet walk up the wall. There comes a point where the elbows have to rotate outward for the chest to move above the hands, and this is best done in a fluid movement. With locked arms pressing down on the hands, a foot can be placed onto the ledge; this allows a step up to be completed but demands considerable leg strength if there are no handholds above the ledge. Hard mantels may require the transfer of the chest from below to above the hands to be made as a jump with no intermediate footholds.

Try to catch the hold at the dead point: This is the point at the apex of the trajectory when the climber is neither moving up nor down. This is only a split second, but with practice the moment begins to feel longer.

LOCK-OFFS, FLAGGING AND EGYPTIAN MOVES

These are all useful techniques for stopping the body from rotating outward when making long reaches on steep rock.

Locking off

A lock-off is simply a fully contracted elbow, allowing the other arm to reach out for a hold. This is a powerful holding position, but it also limits the amount of reach available. The basic lock-off with the hips parallel to the rock face is the classic ladder-climbing style that works well on easy-angled rock but is very inefficient on steep rock, as the shoulder and elbow have to counteract the natural pivoting effect of gravity.

Twist-locks

On steep rock the lock-off becomes far more versatile if the upper body is turned to face the hold. Often this is combined with turning the hips at right angles to the rock by using the outside edge of the opposite foot. The lock-off now places the forearm across the chest and raises the other shoulder up to a full shoulder-width higher, allowing a considerably greater reach.

A powerful lock-off with the arm across the chest allows a much longer reach.

Flagging

Flagging provides a counterbalance for sideways reaches when only one foothold is available. For a long reach left, if the feet point right and one leg is held out horizontally, the weight of the leg and foot counterbalance as the torso begins to lean out beyond the other foot. This keeps the center of gravity above the foothold. Facing the toes away from the direction of travel may feel counterintuitive at first but it is very effective.

Flagging is also a useful way to prevent the upper body from rotating during powerful twist-locks, by providing a lever to hold the pelvis steady. On really steep rock a full twist-lock may require one leg dangling to help force the twist.

Outside flag

The outside flag is the usual application. With the pelvis at right angles to the rock the outer hip is released, allowing that leg to be used for flagging. This feels relatively secure and allows very long reaches to be made.

Inside flag

If the inner leg is used for flagging, this can initially feel precarious. It can help to

TIP

Flagging is particularly effective for maintaining stability when a left-right hand-foot combination is not possible, as it helps prevent barn-door rotation.

Here, flagging with the outside leg helps this climber maintain his delicately balanced position on the sharp edge.

make a long reach possible when a right hand-and-foot combination are required instead of using the familiar opposite hand to opposite foot combination generally advocated in this book. It can also be a useful way to lock off on tiny side pulls on steep rock when it is vital to counteract body rotation.

Flagging with the inside leg allows this climber to initiate a long reach with her left hand. The leverage allows body torque to be maintained.

Dropped knees and Egyptian moves

Dropping a knee requires flexible hips but is one of the most valuable of all techniques for tackling steep rock. Sometimes dropping a knee allows the toe to pull on a hold as the pelvis is being actively rotated outward during a move. Thus the foot initially makes contact with a sidehold with the sole pointing upward, and then rotates as the body

An Egyptian move allows vertical footholds to be used and can take a lot of weight off of the arms when no other footholds are available.

Flagging a leg to give balance as the climber prepares for a long reach.

moves up into a conventional stemming position.

The dropped knee can also be used without rotation during a sequence. This is known as an Egyptian move because of the resemblance to ancient Egyptian figure paintings (it is also sometimes referred to as backstepping). This posture allows the feet to push in opposition, even if using vertical holds. Sometimes this is the only way that either hand can be freed up to place protection, or simply to reach for a hold.

TIP

Egyptian moves are useful in chimneys but equally effective on tufas and flakes on steep walls.

RESTING AND CONSERVING ENERGY

Even the strongest climbers benefit from conserving energy. Anyone can be caught out by an unexpected hard move near the end of the pitch—with no strength reserves there will be nothing left "in the bank" to be used.

Efficient climbing

The techniques described in this book will help you conserve energy. Using left-right opposing limbs on steep rock keeps the main axis passing through the center of gravity and prevents rotation mechanically rather than by wasting strength. Dropped-knee technique and heel hooks take weight from the arms and help pull the center of gravity toward the feet. Solid finger and hand jams allow the limbs to support weight rather than muscular effort.

Pacing

A fundamental way to conserve energy is by varying your speed of movement according to the angle of the rock.

In climbing competitions there is a proven strong correlation between speed of movement and success. On overhanging sections, the faster climbers have the best results, while on technical wall climbs the slow methodical approach pays off the most. This is because on steeper climbs with simple faceholds the main enemy is gravity, so every second counts. On technical wall climbs gravity takes more of a toll if the movement flow is inefficient, so cautious measured movement allows the body to react before a mistake develops into a problem.

Seeking rests

Good climbers will divide a pitch into a series of paced sprints between resting points. Sometimes the planning can be done at ground level; for example, a cave might provide an obvious place to sit or even lie,

so energy can be flooded into a hard move just below without repercussions above.

A resting point before a hard sequence allows practice runs as a rehearsal for the final performance when the first section is climbed efficiently, leaving energy available for the finishing moves. Rather than blasting uncertainly through the opening moves and faltering higher up, it may be possible to scuttle back to the resting place after each reconnaissance. Sometimes it is possible to reverse climb all the way to the ground without having to weight the rope.

Identifying opportunities to recover sets the best climbers apart, and gives an efficient climber the advantage over stronger individuals. There are two kinds of rest:

Good balance allows this climber to keep all weight over the feet and rest both arms.

By moving his backside down this climber **hangs from straight arms**, using the skeleton rather than elbow muscles.

first fall. Knee locks can also allow one or both hands to be freed. Partial recovery can be obtained by varying between horizontal and vertical grips, and by hanging with straight limbs from a good hold.

Shaking out

Full recovery after a complete pump can take several minutes, so don't rush back into the breach too soon. The lactic acid can be dispersed by shaking the hands and forearms gently. The most effective shake-out (known as the G-Tox) alternates 10 seconds below the waist with 10 seconds above to allow assistance from gravity.

> **TIP**
>
> A resting point allows the muscles and tendons to recover and the brain to take stock.

physical and mental. A physical rest allows either all, or specific, limbs to recover and dispel the lactic acid that builds up with continuous exertion. A mental rest brings the level of arousal down to a positive level to allow clear thinking and creative movement.

Mental recovery will vary enormously from person to person and is covered in more detail in *Psychological Preparation* on page 124. Physical rests are also personal—one climber's rest is another person's battle, but the underlying principles apply to everybody. For the upper body, a no-hands rest is ideal for recovery. On less than vertical ground, virtually any ledge might provide this opportunity, while even on steep terrain some contortion of the body around rock bulges might allow the center of gravity to be moved directly over the feet, freeing the hands.

Resting in difficult locations

Rests can often be found even on the most overhanging terrain. Hanging columns or groove walls may allow stemming or even back and foot positions. It may be possible to lock the foot into a pocket and hang upside down, but care is required to avoid a head-

"Shaking out." This climber is dispersing lactic acid by shaking his free hand.

AEROBIC FITNESS AND ENDURANCE

Aerobic fitness

Underlying any specific training regime is the need to maintain a base level of heart and lung efficiency to supply oxygenated blood to the muscles and to remove the waste products of muscle action. Aerobic fitness increases the amount of oxygen that is delivered to your muscles, which allows them to work longer. Compared to many sports, however, climbing does not rely heavily on aerobic fitness, and the main benefit of this type of training comes from fat loss and stress release.

Training techniques

Any activity that raises your heart rate and keeps it up for an extended period of time will improve your aerobic fitness—it is most effective at the level at which you can still conduct a conversation comfortably. This means moderate exercise such as hill walking is an ideal complement to a climber's training and can be used constructively to visit new crags. Gentle running is also very effective, although for upper-body training swimming is a good choice, and continuous movement on easy climbs and scrambles is probably the best and most enjoyable cardiovascular training of all. For weight loss, food intake before light exercise should be just a light snack, as this is when stored fat is broken down to produce energy.

Muscular endurance

Specific muscular endurance is the key to success on long pitches, and can make all the difference for a climber emerging from a crux move onto a sequence of easy but powerful moves. The training goal is to

Steve Monks on the endless dihedral of Ozymandias (28) Mount Buffalo, Australia. On long pitches like this with no resting places, **endurance is vital.**

A heinous heel hooking traverse like this requires **core strength** and the endurance to keep going.

recruit improved oxygen supply and waste dispersal for the muscles by encouraging the body to adapt to regular and increasing demands. For climbers the most obvious effect is postponing the buildup of lactic acid in the muscles, a buildup that is known as getting pumped. Endurance training should involve movement rather than hanging motionless from holds or a bar for long periods, otherwise instead of improving the blood supply the result is more likely to be chronic injuries such as arthritis, varicose veins and tendonitis.

Training techniques

- **Capillary training:** Long traverses or linked climbs flush the muscles with blood and this stimulates the development of denser networks of blood vessels over time. This improves recovery rate and delays the onset of getting pumped.
- **Aerobic training:** For long sustained routes, several sessions per week comprising a variety of lengths and difficulty of climbs will encourage your body to adapt with improved blood supply and efficient energy release.
- **Anaerobic training:** To delay getting pumped on short intense routes (10-move problems and bouldery routes), train on a sequence of progressively difficult routes, finishing right at your limit to recruit improved energy releases, particularly in the larger muscle fibers.
- **Hypergravity training:** Advanced training can incorporate the use of a weighted belt for the above exercises to combine endurance and strength training. To favor endurance keep the weight down to about 10 lb (22 kg).

TAKE NOTE

Anybody with a heart or respiratory condition should consult their doctor before embarking on a fitness-training program, while people who are middle-aged and unaccustomed to exercise should proceed with caution. Climbers feeling "under the weather" with a cold or flu are best advised to lay off training until their resting pulse has returned to normal.

STRENGTH AND POWER

Strength

Climbing requires sufficient strength (the ability to exert force) to transport the body's weight upward against the pull of gravity. Because of the infinite variety of movements and positions required, you should work on opposing muscle groups, such as both the biceps and triceps in the upper arm. Varied training is also more fun and therefore more sustainable, so treat the exercises listed below as a starting point, but remember—you can enjoy climbing without doing any special training. Teenagers in particular should beware the dangers of overtraining, which can have adverse effects on tendons and muscles.

Training

Increases in strength are best achieved by progressive overload. We become stronger by gradually increasing our tolerance to increased demands. However, a sudden increase, especially after time off, is not advised. Free weights and a weight belt are useful tools for strength training. High repetitions with light weights favor endurance, while low repetitions with heavy loads train power.

> ### FINGER BOARDS
>
> These allow specific strength training for fingers and can be made simply from a wooden slat about 1 in (2.5 cm) deep with a rounded front. Manufactured boards are available with various holds. The finger board should be used for short hangs (less than 10 seconds), so if you find it easy, try pull-ups, a weighted belt or different finger combinations—preferably one-handed. If you find finger boards too strenuous, try progressive overloading using bathroom scales to measure the amount of weight your fingers take, gradually increasing to 100 percent.
>
>
>
> Here a finger board has been combined with a pull-up bar in a doorway to allow training for lock-offs and using different sized holds.

Before you start a specific exercise, warm up by running, jumping, hopping, doing push-ups, etc., to get the blood flowing.

Upper body

A classic strength training exercise is the pull-up, using either a metal pull-up bar across a doorway, or a shaped board with various sizes of fingerholds. Be sure to screw in the bar securely. It can be used for a range of exercises, including wide grips, lock-offs (use varying elbow angles), different finger combinations and one-arm work. Try traveling lock-offs: From a wide grip, start

Wrist curls for the biceps: Raise and lower the weight slowly; only the forearm should move.

Weight training for the triceps: From this position hinge the elbow so the forearm hangs vertically and then straighten.

Keep the body straight for push-ups: Add a hand-clap for plyometric power training.

with your chin by one hand and virtually slide it along the bar to the other hand.

TIP

Sets of 20 to 30 hanging leg raises are a fantastic exercise for abs, shoulders and back. Don't cheat by swinging.

Typical steep limestone: Powerful climbing on pinch grips.

If you cannot perform any pull-ups yet, start with chin-ups (knuckles facing away from you), and if that is also too difficult, attach the bar lower so you can perform pull-ups with your toes touching the floor. If you can perform 10 or more pull-ups, try using a weighted belt. These exercises should be performed slowly without swing momentum. Avoid pure strength training on crimps, as these holds will cause tendon damage.

For opposition, work the triceps with a narrow-grip push-up. Place your hands near the ribcage base, touching your chest. Elbows should be kept close to the body during the push-ups and slow lowers. This can be eased by keeping knees on the floor, or toughened by putting the feet on a step.

For all pull-up work, descent must be controlled, to avoid dropping onto a straight elbow—a common cause of injuries.

Lower body

Squats and heel raises, with or without weights, are great for building thigh strength. Squat thrusts are also excellent and help develop balance.

Power

This is what might be termed explosive strength—the ability to exert force dynamically. For bouldering and hard

crux moves, power is vital for dynamic moves and long reaches from poor holds. The fast-twitch fibers needed for power decline with age, but training significantly offsets this deterioration.

Training

Proper warm-ups are again essential. Power exercises should lead to muscle failure after about five repetitions (or about eight moves for each hand) on a climb. Useful top-rope exercises include speed climbing, and eliminating moves from a climb so that a series of dynos is required. Exercises such as push-ups can be modified for power by adding a hand-clap at each extension.

One-armed traverses across walls and hands-only climbing on overhanging terrain are excellent training for a combination of body tension, speed and power.

For power, focus on short, hard problems— big moves on steep rock.

STRENGTH AND POWER

BUILDING CORE STRENGTH
Core strength is vital to climbers for controlling the body tension that is essential for the hands and feet to work in unison.

Fitness ball
Regular use of a fitness ball will make a significant difference to your core strength and balance, even if only used to watch TV or sit at a computer. Sit upright on a firmly inflated ball, with your back straight and your knee joints forming a right angle: your stomach and thighs will make constant tiny balance movements. Dozens of exercises are possible, including single leg raises and abdominal crunches. It can also introduce an element of balance to weight training.

Slacklining
Walking a low slackline (a webbing or rope suspended horizontally), or even a railing is superb training for core strength, and balance awareness. Use your abdomen rather than the shoulders to retain your center of gravity over the weighted foot. The line should be set below groin height to reduce injury potential.

A simple leg raise on a fitness ball: Concentrate on lifting the leg without wobbling.

Sit-ups using a fitness ball are great for balance as well as for building abdominal strength.

Push-ups using a fitness ball are a great way to work both arms equally.

TIP
It is important to balance your training with appropriate rest (longer after heavier sessions) and to recognize early signs of chronic injuries in order to allow sufficient recovery. Fingers are particularly susceptible to injuries and may take years of gradual acclimatization to adapt to the demands hard climbing places on them. Build up gradually, and don't overdo it.

Advanced power training

System training

A safe and enjoyable form of isolation training that requires a specialized panel to be constructed. Identical handholds are attached up a steep panel, ideally about 45° overhanging with positive footholds. Power up and down the wall; grip failure should be after 10 to 20 hand movements. Any type of grip can be worked on using this system, and the footholds make it more relevant to most climbing movement. Once you get stronger a weighted belt (10–20 lb or 4.5–9 kg) can be added for HIT (hypergravity isolation training)—arguably the most effective technique for improving power.

Bachar ladder

This is a rope ladder tensioned between 20° and 30° past vertical and basically involves climbing up the underside. Ape footlessly

up and down the ladder, without allowing hands to share a rung. This trains both power reaches and lock-offs, and also builds both pushing and pulling muscles. If this is too hard, share rungs briefly, or let a foot take some weight.

Campus board

A specialized resource for strong and technically advanced climbers only; it is also the fastest way to damage your arms if you overdo it. The board needs to be at least 2 ft (60 cm) wide (preferably wider to allow different types of rungs). It should overhang by between 10° and 20° to allow leg room, and measure about 8 ft (2.5 m) high, i.e., normal ceiling height. Put plenty of padding underneath.

You can space rungs uniformly at about half-forearm-length apart, or vary the distances; uniform spacing and size keeps the training more specific and recordable. Short sessions of campus boarding within a training program can be used once a week, building to two or three weekly sessions for up to two months, and then phased into less stressful training. In addition to power, this equipment improves dynamic timing, contact finger strength and static strength. Keep sessions short and only do it when you are feeling fresh.

- **Laddering:** Use the rungs like a Bachar ladder, but work for the longest reach to improve **dead pointing**.
- **Double-dynos and plyometrics:** Leap both hands simultaneously to a higher or lower rung. For plyometrics, double-dyno down a rung and then back up as quickly as possible; the speed of turnaround is important.

A full-sized campus board in a gym: Different sized rungs and different spacings can clearly be seen. This board can be used for a variety of exercises, including dynos and plyometrics. Use with care.

FLEXIBILITY

Training for strength alone has a detrimental effect on mobility, and should always be balanced by a program of stretching. Muscles are a series of interconnecting fibers that contract and relax in order to move. Regularly stretching a joint just beyond its normal working limit will encourage an increase in the range of movement. A good range of movement in all the body's joints allows available strength to be applied most effectively and permits awkward combinations of holds to be performed without undue discomfort. Passive stretching before each workout helps prevent injuries and regains the level of flexibility you had at the end of a previous workout; it will also help reduce the tightening of muscles as you recover.

Training

As with all areas of training, the body reacts to regular demands, so frequent sessions of gentle stretching are far better than a weekly (or monthly) blowout. Stretching muscles, ligaments and tendons beyond their normal limits is potentially dangerous, so make sure you warm up thoroughly before starting to stretch, preferably in a warm room. Below are some general stretches as well as some that increase flexibility in specific areas. Avoid "bouncing" into the stretch.

General limb stretches

- **Passive stretching:** Stretch until you feel your limb is at full stretch (the "end" position), and hold that position for about 20 seconds. Now push a bit further and hold the new position for 10 seconds. Maintain this cycle for up to 10 minutes. With regular practice your original "end" position will gradually extend.

- **Isometric resistance:** Get a partner to hold your limb in the "end" position while you attempt, with all your strength, to pull back. This isometric contraction should be held for about six seconds. Allow the limb to relax, and then your partner should be able to extend your "end" position a little. Repeat this three or four times and then rest. This technique is effective but

Forearm stretch: With hands in the "prayer" position close to the chest, rotate them down.

Triceps stretch: Pull the elbow behind the head.

Shoulder stretch: Use a forearm to pull the straight arm closer to the chest.

Upper back stretch: Clasp fingers and push forward with elbows soft.

TIP

Consider cross-training.
Practicing martial arts or yoga
will help provide the discipline
required to stretch properly.

Work the **antagonistic muscles**
with this lower back stretch.

Abdominal stretch: Keep the
thighs touching the ground
and push the shoulders up.

potentially injurious the first time and
it is therefore imperative that you stop
if it hurts.

Forearms

- Adopt a "prayer" position with the hands
  together. Keeping the elbows horizontal
  and the palms together, rotate the hands
  slowly toward and away from the chest.
- Put one hand flat on a wall with the
  fingers horizontal and the arm straight.
  Ease your body in the direction that the
  fingers point until keeping the palm on the
  wall becomes an effort. Repeat with the
  fingers pointing in the opposite direction.

Triceps

- With one elbow behind your head with
  the hand behind its opposite shoulder, use
  the other hand to pull your elbow gently
  downward. If this is easy, try gripping
  your hands together behind your back and
  gently pull. Use a towel to link your hands
  if they don't meet.

Back and abdomen

- **Abdomen:** Lie on your front and, while
  keeping your hips on the floor, slowly
  extend your arms, curving your torso off
  the floor, until you feel a good stretch
  along the front of your body.
- **Upper back:** Hold a pull-up bar with
  your feet directly below and lean forward.
  Alternatively, raise your elbows and
  forearms in a "hands up, surrender"
  posture on the walls on either side of
  a doorframe and lean forward.

Legs

- **Hamstrings:** Sit with legs apart and knees
  slightly bent. Bend your chest toward one
  leg, straighten, rotate and bend between
  the legs, then straighten and bend toward
  the other leg. Keep your chin up
  so your back stays straight.
- **Thighs:** Sit with your feet
  together and your elbows
  between your knees. Grasp
  your ankles and lever your
  knees out using your elbows.

Groin stretch—very useful for
"frogging" moves. Grasp the
ankles with soles of the feet
together. Use elbows to
ease knees down.

Calf stretch:
Lower one heel
off a step while
pushing your
knees forward.

Hamstring stretch: Resist the
temptation to reach further by curving
your back. Keep the head upright.

TRAINING SCHEDULES AND NUTRITION

This is a basic, jargon-free introduction to a complex subject. The starting point of any training schedule is to take a long, hard appraisal of your strengths and weaknesses. Decide on your short-, medium- and long-term goals—perhaps a checklist of routes, or reaching a specific grade. These goals should be realistic for your lifestyle or you must decide what changes you are prepared to make. If you want to climb harder routes, then regular exercise is necessary, otherwise you will plateau or sustain injuries—perhaps both. For most climbers the best and most enjoyable training simply involves a regular and varied climbing schedule.

Find training partners
Training is a lot more fun if somebody with similar or complementary goals can share it with you. You can learn from each other, spark some competition and protect each

other from injuries. A regular climbing partner will share successes, tolerate the occasional long belaying stint and provide moral support for your big leads.

Periodized training
Indoor climbers can structure training around a simple cycle of progression to a climax followed by recovery and further development. Each session should start within your present comfort zone, and the timing of cycle peaks may need to be tailored to climbing competitions. Outdoor climbers have to contend with the seasonal and regional climate as well as variable weather, so a flexible plan based around these variations is required, building to a peak before climbing breaks. A regular lifestyle and vacations booked well in advance, plus occasional visits to a climbing gym, makes this discipline easier to achieve.

Recovery
Regular exercise stimulates the physical development that occurs during intermediate rest. If the rest periods are too short, the muscles may become cannibalized for protein; if too long, the stimulus to develop is lost. Full rest for several days is required after heavy strength sessions or minor injuries, but otherwise "active rest" is excellent, preferably with contrasting or complementary activity.

Schedule
Here is one simple training cycle that builds strength, power and then endurance, with continuous development of technique to construct efficient brain-to-limb memory patterns (engrams). Many specialized variations are possible.

Bouldering is a social activity that is a great way to encourage **healthy competition** while at the same time providing a supportive atmosphere.

Healthy food choices: Carbohydrates taken before and after a climb will help keep your energy levels up, but don't climb on a full stomach, particularly with dairy products such as milk and cheese.

- **Weekend warrior:** Strength/power on Tuesday, endurance on Thursday and cragging on the weekend (power routes on Saturday, easier endurance on Sunday). Be sure to include core strength training and exercises for general fitness such as hill walking or jogging.

Nutrition

An active climbing lifestyle will allow most people to enjoy their food without putting on weight; increasing exercise is a healthier way to lose weight than cutting out food. Here are a few simple tips, but you should consult a specialist if you have problems with nutrition. A balanced diet comprising a good supply of vitamins and fiber, with reduced fat and salt intake, should be your aim.

- Replace the traditional three square meals with smaller portions, linked with healthy snacks such as fruits, vegetables and unsalted nuts to spread your energy intake/processing more effectively. Feeling bloated is no way to start a climb.

- Choose carbohydrate-rich foods like pasta, bread, rice and baked potatoes, with at least five portions of vegetables and fruits per day.
- Snack before, and try to eat within an hour of completing a training session, but avoid a large meal shortly before going to bed. Instead, have a light meal and then a larger breakfast.

Hydration

Drink little and often throughout the day, but avoid carbonated drinks—these cause indigestion and delayed rehydration. You should arrive at a session fully hydrated, and continue drinking modest amounts. Dehydration not only impairs performance but invites soft-tissue injuries, while severe dehydration can be fatal. Hard exercise will require 32 oz (1 L) per hour or even more.

> **TIP**
>
> Try cutting down on dairy products if you suffer from indigestion.

PSYCHOLOGICAL PREPARATION

Although fitness and technique are essential prerequisites for hard climbs, without the right attitude a climber will not be able to capitalize on these assets. Attitude is the key to climbing and it can halt a strong, technical climber completely, just as certainly as it can propel a relatively weak, clumsy climber to the top of the same pitch. Within this enigma lies much of the charm and mystique of the sport.

Motivation

This fuels the desire to succeed, but its source varies in every individual. Honest reflection about your own desires will help you focus on what you really want. Motivation can stem from positive thoughts or negative fears, but

Focus on how good it will feel to grab that finishing hold. Sion Idwal Long gets the final jugs at the end of a 165 ft (50 m) pitch on Quan es sa Fosc (5) in Mallorca.

both success and failure are often linked to self-fulfilling prophecies.

Desire for success
This may be for recognition, fame, money or a desire to achieve potential. Honest acceptance of these desires can help a climber focus on success, but beware of using the reward of progressing to a harder climb as motivation—focus only on the job at hand.

Fear of failure
This demotivator is all too common and may linger after a bad experience or in people with low self-esteem. Some people choose never to put in 100 percent effort because that always leaves one last excuse for failure. Some people fear tarnishing the experience if a climb is completed in less than perfect style, or fear getting committed beyond the protection points and running out of steam.

Fear of success

Some people are genuinely shy of attention and do not perform well in front of a crowd or if expectations are high. Others fear the hollow feeling that comes from completing a project, or worry that completing one move may bring insurmountable difficulties a long way beyond protection.

Relaxation

Stress is a natural element in any endeavor and a healthy level brings a productive state of arousal and anticipation. Too much stress brings anxiety that poisons the brain and leads to poor decision-making and reverting to entrenched bad habits. Learning to relax is a skill climbers can learn to develop in order to keep stress at a productive level.

This climber is **mentally rehearsing** a sequence of moves before leaving the ground.

Breathing control

Feeding the brain and tissues with oxygen using strong, deep breaths offsets the physiological causes of stress and prepares the muscles for action. Concentrating on deep, regular "belly" breathing is a simple and well-documented strategy, and should be essential preparation for any difficult climbing sequence.

Positive visualization

Count your blessings. List only the positive factors, such as your recent successes, how good the top hold will feel and the double-checks of your harness and belayer. Use superstitions like lucky clothing or a favorite extender to your advantage. If a foot slips, remind yourself why that won't happen again. If psychological protection helps you, use it. Use keywords or favorite thoughts to promote well-being and practice these techniques—they can be honed like any other skill.

Eliminate fears

The negative motivators listed above can all be diminished by adequate preparation.

Many fears can be reduced by progressive desensitization—a classic example is the fear of falling. Practice controlled falling in a safe environment and eventually you will cease to fear it, and also learn to fall more safely, so that the actual as well as perceived risk is reduced. Like any other learned skill, this has to be practiced intensively and regularly to become ingrained and remain dominant in times of stress.

Mental preparation

Embark on a training program to build confidence and undermine fears: Work on your weaknesses and play to your strengths. Record your present climbing level and list your short-, medium- and long-term goals, then record milestones so you can regain confidence when stuck on a skills plateau. Break up both your training program and individual climbs into manageable chunks, and mentally rehearse each stage before committing yourself. Break out of a negative spiral by stepping down several grades and really cruising routes for a while.

DEVELOPING STYLE
WITH JOHN DUNNE

John Dunne is one of the strongest and most notorious climbers in the world. He is infamous for pushing climbing grades into new realms of difficulty, including classic routes that are rarely repeated because of their potentially fatal nature. His occasionally controversial climbing career has seen him regularly dominate the headlines over the last 20 years with both traditional (trad) and bolted cutting-edge routes. Of his many first ascents, New Statesman (E8/9 7a) and Parthian Shot (E9 7a) have passed into the realms of legend and awaited repeat ascents for many years. Since 2003, John has worked toward building what is now a thriving business, the Manchester Climbing Centre, in England.

How did you learn to climb so well?
I started as a young mountaineer and realized that I was quite a good rock climber. I consciously developed my footwork. When I found I couldn't jam, or I wasn't very good at laybacking, I worked specifically on these weak points. I was willing to bumble around and fall off stuff until I had the basics mastered, and that is a really hard challenge. It's a big bash on the ego but it's the best grounding you can take in any walk of life. If people can accept that, they're going to be better not just at climbing but in everything they do.

What advice would you give to ambitious novice climbers?
Don't get obsessed by working your way through the grades, just get out and play on the rock. A lot of new climbers haven't gone through the tradition of easy routes in the hills or the gritstone crags—they are coming in quite steep training walls and gaining a lot of strength and fitness very quickly, but missing a lot of the basic techniques. In any sport, if you take a group of youngsters and coach them to be athletes, you should start with a thorough grounding in very basic skills.

So what do you mean by "the basics"?
I mean the ability to "read" the rock and develop fluid movement: linking eye to foot to hand, and just moving in a style that's unique to your build—size and shape—and developing a natural, flowing movement. There's no set way to become a good climber, no set way to move; it's all about shape and size. That often gets forgotten about in training articles—that baseline understanding is what people need to do before they progress to campus boards and desperately hard stuff. Structured training is pointless until you have excellent technique.

John Dunne on one of his many **technical test pieces**: The Great Escape, Arran (Scotland). Weighing in at E8 6c, this fierce trad climb demands good footwork.

So how can somebody discover what their personal style actually is?

The best way to learn in any sport is to dilute it down to a very simple level so you're not stressing your body. Nice, easy climbs with big holds will let you move intuitively; you're not stopping to think, you're just doing it. Looking back at my career as a climber, I went through every grade and did perhaps 50 routes at each level before moving on. Often now you get people who jump from E1 to E4 to E7 but they might struggle on a V.Diff (5.3) chimney because they are too specialized.

But how can people develop this if they are already climbing middle-grade routes?

Take my computer skills: I'm doing quite advanced tasks, yet I don't know my way around the keyboard. I just wish I could start again and just go from A to B to C to D but it's hard to go back when you're already at C. Many people's perception of developing is very grade-oriented; it's all about linear progression. Go and have some fun on some easy classics.

So what is your personal style?

Being a big guy I need to get the weight off my arms and onto my feet, so footwork plays a massive part. Sometimes, even now, I see world-class climbers who weigh 120 lb (55 kg), and think, "If only you used your feet, the sky would be the limit!" So for me a genetic disadvantage has proved to be a strength in the long run.

As a coach what would you recommend that people aspire to?

The best climbers move effortlessly—it's like running a car for as many miles as possible with what's in the tank. That to me is what makes a really good climber: efficiency.

And finally, what would you say to people who don't want to climb any harder?

If you can climb at a modest grade, you

John Dunne powering up the intimidating finger-locks classic; London Wall (E5 6a) at England's Millstone Edge. **Strength and technique** are required in equal measure on this unforgiving classic.

can go anywhere in the world. You can get to the top of most things by an easy or a hard route, so you can have all of the best experiences: friendship, traveling, views, bivouacking, but you'll get there by a different route.

LEARN FROM EXPERIENCE
WITH JIM DONINI

Jim Donini is one of the most respected pioneering climbers in the world, credited with outstanding first ascents on most continents. A founder of the American Mountain Guides Association (AMGA), Jim was awarded the prestigious Underhill Award for outstanding mountaineering achievement by the American Alpine Club (AAC) and went on to become president of the AAC in 2005. His cutting-edge first ascents include Torre Egger (1976), Latok I (1978) and, in Alaska, The Diamond Arête on Mt. Hunter (1985), Cobra Pillar, Mt. Barille (1988), South Face, Mt. Bradley (1994) and Shaken not Stirred on the Moose's Tooth (1997). Jim has continued to make first ascents in Patagonia, and in 2006 came close to success with a bold new line on Fitzroy.

What is the American Alpine Club?

Most nations have their own alpine club to support climbers and protect the mountains, and the U.S. joined this tradition as long ago as 1902. It's for everybody who believes that our climbing heritage and playgrounds need to be protected. It has a world-class library and annual journal and it also organizes rescue insurance, social events and climbing meets, with local sections all over the nation. It's been a real privilege to join a management team that cares so passionately about climbing and also has the practical skills to help the club develop.

When did you first start climbing?

When I left the army in my mid-20s, my buddy and I traveled west. We stopped off in Glacier National Park, saw the mountains, and for me it was obvious: They are there to be climbed! That was in about 1967. We read an early copy of *Mountaineering: The Freedom of the Hills*, got some money together and bought some climbing gear. My partner was afraid of heights, so I led my very first climbs—I wouldn't recommend that, though! Now you can learn in a much more structured way, but that was in the 1960s and you just had to work it out for yourself.

Yosemite was where things were happening, so I headed there. It's the perfect venue for crack climbing, so that's what I started with, before I learned to face climb. It was the ideal apprenticeship because in the alpine environment you need cracks to place your own gear, so you're always following crack lines.

So what is the secret to climbing cracks?

Practice! It's all about efficient movement, going quickly and smoothly, and using less energy. I don't take those gloves or anything fancy, I just wind the tape around my hands

Famed for its fickle weather, **Fitzroy** is currently the object of Jim Donini's attentions. The Patagonian veteran has his sights set on completing a new line climbed in the purest of styles.

Jim leading at the **Splitter Camps**, his famous crack climbing courses at Indian Creek, Utah.

mountains, but you could fill a book with our adventures! One member of the team, Rab Carrington, learned how to make sleeping bags during the journey, but that's another story. I still climb with him sometimes, though.

How have you and your contemporaries managed to continue climbing at such a high standard for so long?
Partly genetics, but mostly it's about still being interested. It's not a sport that has to rely on reflexes or speed, where if you lose a bit, you can't be competitive. Climbing requires strength, endurance, technique, knowledge and experience, and most of those grow with you. Even endurance and strength stay with you quite well. I can't climb after a night's partying like I used to. I have to prepare more and take better care of myself now, but I'm still trying to push the envelope a little bit, seeing what my limits are.

What style of climbing do you aspire to?
With modern gear we have so many advantages that I'm always trying to climb better and harder than I used to. Climbing is about doing things with the minimum amount of technological support. When I hear about people placing bolts next to crack lines in Patagonia, it makes me sad. You could, by using technological support, overcome just about any obstacle but that's not what climbing is about. Radios, bolt belays, oxygen ... they all undermine commitment and give a false sense of security. It's easy to say these things make climbing more convenient but I believe they detract from the experience. If I can't hang on and place protection for myself, I'd rather leave it for the next generation. Reinhold Messner was right: We shouldn't murder the impossible, we should just get better!

a few times and I'm done. I like to look at where I'm going and go for that spot without stopping a lot to put too much gear in. The more you stop and hang around, the more pumped you're going to feel. With crack climbing, failure comes because endurance goes, rarely because a move is too difficult. I still get a real kick out of my involvement with the Splitter Camps at Indian Creek in Utah, where we teach people how to jam in one of the world's most special places.

When did you start climbing hard routes on big, remote mountains?
In 1974. My first climbing had been in the mountains and I'd done a fair bit of big wall climbing in Yosemite. I started hearing about Patagonia, the southern tip of South America, so I went out there on a whim with a friend of mine. We nearly managed the first ascent of Cerro Stanhardt; in fact we would have, except our stove stopped working and we had to go down to replace it. When we went back, the window of good weather had closed, but we got very near the summit anyway. The next year we made it up a magnificent mountain, the unclimbed plum, Torre Egger.

One early trip to Patagonia with a bunch of Brits was such an epic that after months of travel, we never got all our gear to the

CLIMBING TRIPS
WITH JEREMY COLENSO AND RACHEL KELSEY

Jeremy Colenso and Rachel Kelsey both won South African national championship titles in sport climbing in the 1990s. They subsequently competed internationally in climbing and adventure climbing (in the World Cup and Eco Challenge). Rachel was the first of only four women in the world to go through the British Forces 21 SAS selection course. For 14 years Jeremy's One Flew Over the Cuckoo's Nest climb (1991, six pitches at 30) was unrepeated and arguably the hardest trad climb on the African continent. They share a passion for climbing and leading expeditions in extreme or remote locations where physical and mental boundaries are pushed to the limit. Here they give us their advice on climbing trips.

How do you get the best out of a trip?
We train regularly and specifically for what we are intending to do. For a sport climbing trip we will focus on training for similar climbs. For more ambitious trips we devise

Jeremy Colenso enjoying an easy winter climb on **Snowdon's Trinity Face** in North Wales.

methods to move quickly and safely over the terrain, and practice any specialized techniques such as hauling before we go. Climbing at altitude or in heat requires acclimatization, which normally has to wait until you arrive, so you have to factor this into the time scale of your trip.

What do you eat when you're traveling?
We take high-performance carbohydrate drinks for extended climbs. This keeps you hydrated and fed without losing any time when speed is important. We use our multi-fuel stove because it works better at altitude and in extreme cold. We generally carry two stacked pots so one can cook vegetables or boil water for tea, on top of the other, which cooks rice or potatoes.

How do you stay healthy on the road/ flight?
We take as many creature comforts as we can, for example a good inflatable foam mat or mattress, and a warm sleeping bag. If using a bivvy bag, make sure that it is waterproof and breathable. For car camping take chairs, a table and a good-sized towel for showering. We try to fly direct on long-haul routes.

How do you look after valuables?
In parts of the U.S. we use animal-proof safes rather than leaving edibles (including toothpaste) in the car. Where crime is a problem, we take everything out of the car and hide it in an inaccessible area covered in natural foliage, and leave the car unlocked with the windows down and the dashboard open to signify to potential opportunist thieves that there is nothing of value in the vehicle. We also use more than one steering-wheel locking device as a deterrent.

In Europe, official campsites are generally fairly safe for most items, although we

Rachel on **Table Mountain, South Africa,** where she first developed her climbing skills.

sometimes carry our passports and bank cards with us in waterproof bags, especially where proof of identity is required. Family campsites are often a good option because the neighboring family will keep an eye on your belongings when you are off climbing. If reception at a gîte or campsite has a safe, we use it.

What's your favorite destination?
Jeremy: Ceuse, France—great climbing and fantastic views. The Italian Alps and Cedarburg for adventure.
Rachel: Tibet, just outside Lhasa, sport climbing at altitude in a bizarre, traditional setting. Spitzkoppe in the Namib desert— amazing views and fantastic memories. We like being in remote areas where we have to rely on our skills and experience.

What equipment do you carry with you?
For alpine climbing, we share a sleeping bag and always carry a reliable ultra-light survival shelter—this has saved our bacon more than once. Our ropes are light and dry-treated: wet or frozen ropes are just an extra hazard in a storm. Along with spare hat and gloves we carry a map and compass and a fully charged phone. Minimal first-aid kit (bandages, steristrips, cotton pads for extreme bleeding, and an EpiPen for my allergy to bee stings) along with expertise from an advanced first-aid course. We pack head lamps even when bouldering.

How do you deal with hot conditions?
We grew up in a hot climate and seem to be more adapted to hot, dry conditions, but vice versa, we have to take more precautions in extreme cold. We are disciplined about water intake and use long-sleeved, pale clothing plus high-factor skin protection against the sun. On the north face of Half Dome (Yosemite, California) we limited our water intake to 1¾ gal (7 L) between us for the entire climb. For speed we pulled on the occasional piece of protection during the climb (25 pitches at 5.11 and 5.12) rather than haul enough gear to spend time working moves. We took two days, and by planning where the sun would be we were able to stay mostly in the shade.

RIGGING A RAPPEL

Rappelling is a method of creating sufficient friction on the rope to make a controlled descent of steep or even overhanging terrain. It is an important mountaineering skill, but is also taught and practiced as an activity in its own right.

Rappelling allows the descent of rock faces that would be too dangerous or time-consuming to descend on foot, and is also an important component of any climber's problem-solving repertoire for escaping from crags or evacuating a person who has become stuck on a crag for any reason.

Practice sites

An important consideration for choosing a practice site is avoiding damage to existing rock climbs or sensitive vegetation. The landowner or facility manager's permission may be needed and, for manufactured structures, an engineer's report is highly recommended to confirm structural stability and suitability of anchors.

For novices the ideal practice site is a smooth slab or wall, with no ledges to break

The rope to be retrieved (red in this case) has been threaded under the anchor sling so that it is **not locked against the rock** when pulled down. A simple overhand knot connects the rope ends.

the flow, and no overhangs to negotiate. The crag and takeoff point must be stable to prevent material from being dislodged. An unimpeded view from the top to the foot of the crag is also highly desirable. The most intimidating part of a rappel is getting established at the edge of the cliff, so a good takeoff point is helpful, with the anchor point ideally above waist height so the rope provides good support as the rappeller learns to trust the rope. Low anchors mean the rope lies along the ground, making the takeoff difficult and intimidating.

Anchors

For rappelling the rope must be attached securely to a sound belay—the same credentials as for a climbing belay, so follow the START guidelines described in *Constructing Safe Belays* on page 60. In a single-pitch setting the rope can usually be fastened directly to the belay. For longer descents it is often necessary to retrieve the rope after each rappel. This requires a doubled rope to be threaded through the anchor point, probably a webbing or metal ring linking anchors.

This climber has attached himself to an anchor using a sling arranged as a cow's tail.

An anchor that is higher than the rappeller's waist level is pulled downward rather than outward, and allows a comfortable, straightforward start.

To connect two ropes a simple overhand knot tied about 2 ft (less than 1 m) from the rope ends is very effective and less prone to jamming on edges than other knots. Don't use a figure-eight knot as it slips undone when the two ends are pulled apart. Having clipped into the next belay point with a sling girth-hitched to the harness, one end of the rope is pulled down. This needs to be the end on the knotted side at the anchor, so check this before rappelling. It will be retrieved more freely if this end is on the "inside" of the rappel sling, i.e., touching the rock. When the end is pulled, this prevents the sling from crushing against the other end and locking it.

Roped descents rely on sound anchors and careful checks of all attachments. If any component of the system becomes detached, the consequences could be disastrous—rappelling has caused more serious injuries than any other mountaineering activity. The belay bears all of the loading, and can be shock-loaded if the rappeller slips or leaps past an overlap, so an inadequate belay negates the entire system. To avoid needless strain, rappel descents should be steady and avoid sudden drops (despite the popular television image of the commando-style descent).

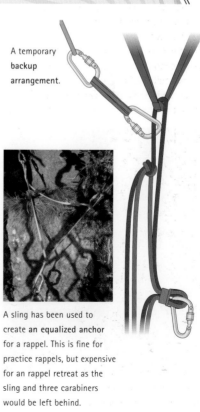

A temporary backup arrangement.

A sling has been used to create an equalized anchor for a rappel. This is fine for practice rappels, but expensive for an rappel retreat as the sling and three carabiners would be left behind.

DESCENDING THE ROPE

Rappel technique

Controlling the speed of descent is allowed by threading the rappel rope through either a belay device or a "figure-eight" descendeur. Descendeurs are heavy so are mainly used only for group rappelling.

The rappel device should be securely attached to the harness with a locking carabiner. Climbing harnesses are designed with rappelling as a secondary function, but most have a tape loop connecting the leg loops to the waist belt, generally referred to as the "rappel loop." Clipping a single point like this helps prevent a three-way loading, i.e., tension at both ends of the back bar and also across the gate. This reduces the strength of the carabiner, but also dramatically increases the chances of the gate opening, especially with a figure-eight device.

The rappeller gradually leans back until the spine is in a fairly vertical position, with the rappel device supporting the full body weight and the control hand pulling the rope away from the live rope to maximize friction in exactly the same way as in halting

> **TIP**
>
> Let the rappel device do the work of providing friction by holding onto the brake rope below the rappel equipment. Novices sometimes panic and grab the live rope with both hands, negating the effect of the equipment—so beginners may benefit from using both hands to hold the brake end of the rope.

a fall. This feels more natural for climbers who are already familiar with using the device for belaying.

Safety backup

For practicing rappels a safety rope backup fastened directly to the rappeller's harness is highly recommended. An ordinary climbing rope is normally used for the backup safety rope. For group sessions this is most conveniently controlled using a direct belay either attached to a separate belay, or clipped into the same equalized attachment loop(s) as the rappel rope. In an emergency this rope can easily be locked while the problem is solved.

Experienced climbers will often find it

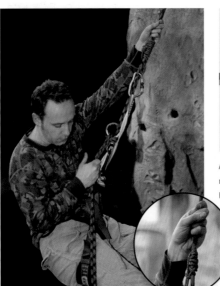

Above: **An autoblock** has been placed below the rappel device and clipped to a securely buckled leg loop. Make sure that the autoblock cannot touch the belay device.

Left: Rappelling with **a prusik backup** above the belay device. The sling should be less than arm's length.

A classic prusik: Start by making a girth hitch around the rope and then pass the loop through again once or twice. Pull tight, keeping the knot symmetrical.

The second type of prusik is called an autoblock. Simply wrap the thin rope loop around the main rope four or five times and clip the ends together.

necessary to rappel without an additional backup rope, but a failsafe system is still highly recommended in case the grip on the brake rope fails for any reason—perhaps due to injuries. While a partner can provide a degree of emergency braking by pulling hard on the brake rope from the bottom of the rappel, a more reliable method is for the rappeller to control a clutch system, which will lock if their hand releases it. A prusik hitch attached around the brake end of the rope and fastened to the harness leg loop generally provides the most effective protection. While the prusik is held loosely by the brake hand, it allows the rope to slide through the rappel device. If the hand is released, however, the prusik locks onto the rope and acts as a "dead-man's hand" firmly gripping the rope. The locked prusik must not be allowed to touch the device or a projection from the rock because this might cause it to release.

Some people prefer to attach a prusik above the rappel point and attach this to the harness with a sling. This works well as long as the prusik can be reached with a bent elbow, or it can jam up beyond reach.

Rappelling with a safety line as backup is highly recommended for novices. In this situation an instructor may fasten the rappel rope to the anchor using a Münter hitch, so that the attachment can be released if any problems arise, allowing the rappeller to be simply lowered to the ground using the safety line.

SAFETY PROCEDURES FOR RAPPELLING

Rappelling is inherently more dangerous than climbing because loading the system is unavoidable. Manage the risk by working through these procedures.

Anchor checks

Don't assume that in situ anchors are sound just because they have been used before. Check for signs of corrosion, fractures and movement. Check slings for signs of abrasion; pulling rope through a sling after rappelling generates a lot of friction, and sometimes enough heat to burn right through the sling after completing just one rappel.

Don't take risks to save money. Carry some cord and a carabiner you don't mind sacrificing so you can create a new anchor at the top (this would be left behind when you rappel down), or just throw some brand-new gear at the problem. How much is your life worth? If you do not have enough gear to leave much equipment behind, arrange a temporary backup by setting up failsafe secondary anchors left slightly slack so the main anchor is definitely taking the entire load. Send the heaviest person down first, and watch the anchor very carefully.

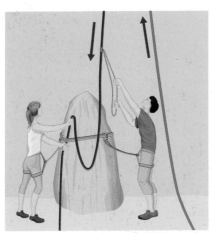

> **TIP**
>
> If you don't have complete faith in the rappel system, change something.

If satisfied, strip the backups and follow on down very carefully, minimizing bounce. Take care not to pull outward on a blunt spike, especially while getting established for a rappel. If necessary, belly-flop off of the ledge to keep the loading as close to vertical as possible. For multi-pitch rappels, don't continue past a possible anchor point without checking that there is another station before the end of the rope. Failure to do this will result in either having to sacrifice equipment unnecessarily or having to prusik back up the rope.

Tie knots in the rope ends

Unless you can see that the rope touches the ground, tie a stopper knot in the bottom end of the rope to stop you from rappelling off the end. Leave a couple of feet of rope beyond the knot so it can't creep off the end of the rope if weighted.

If you are rappelling on doubled ropes, a separate knot for each is generally less likely to snag, but undo the knots before you try to retrieve the ropes.

Friction

If ropes are threaded directly through a webbing sling and allowed to slide under load (common with ropes of different thicknesses or ages), this can very quickly melt right through the sling.

> **TIP**
>
> If it is possible to leave a rope in place when you rappel in to climb a route, do so. If things go wrong it might be your only way back out.

If the rope is difficult to retrieve and you are not able to walk away from the cliff base to reduce friction, try **attaching a prusik** to the rope and use this as a handhold. Clip into the anchor in case it releases unexpectedly.

Use a carabiner to link the ropes to the anchor if you see this as a potential problem. If you are short of carabiners, butt the knot connecting the ropes right up against the sling, passing the thinner rope through. This prevents the rope from slipping, because the rope is already in the position it would slide to.

All devices provide less friction when used with brand-new rope(s), and the thinner the rope, the less friction is provided.

Stacked rappel

If rappelling with inexperienced climbers, before you leave you can set everybody's rappel systems up on the rope and release your partners from any cow's-tail connections to the belay. For comfort, attach the belay device to a short sling so the person at the stance is not pulled around too much by the rappeller. As long as your weight is on the rope they will not be able to set off from the stance. Provide safety cover by pulling the ropes hard if a descending partner lets go of the rope.

Above: A **stacked rappel** is used to protect less experienced rappellers. The leader has lined up three people ready to rappel and can provide some safety backup by pulling the ropes if anybody begins to descend too fast. Notice that there is nothing left for the people on the ledge to unfasten, minimizing the opportunities for confusion.

Right: For **multi-pitch rappels** tie a knot at the end of each rope if you cannot be certain that they reach the ground.

ASCENDING A ROPE

Rope-climbing skills are most likely to be needed when rappelling. Once you are committed to a descent, if problems arise such as rappelling the wrong line or failure to climb out, re-ascending via the rappel rope may be the only way out. This option is only available of course if the rappel rope has been left in place.

This is a potentially dangerous activity as it loads the system, and can easily cause rope abrasion from rock edges. Before starting to climb a rope you should make a thorough risk assessment, starting from the standpoint that an alternative solution such as an easy climb is usually preferable.

Equipment

To ascend a rope, two sliding clutches are needed. For an unplanned evacuation these will probably be two of the prusik loops that you should carry on your harness at all times. Some people carry light gadgets such as Tiblocs or Ropemen for this contingency. For sea-cliff approach rappels and for following aid pitches you might choose to carry mechanical devices such as jumars. If these are only carried for emergencies, they can be left attached to the rappel rope while you climb. If prusik loops are used, avoid using two autoblocks as these can sometimes slide downward, and if the top one slips, it will take the lower loop with it. The Kleimheist is recommended for the

This climber is using **two prusiks**, with a long sling fixed to the bottom prusik as a foot stirrup. The sling in this picture looks slightly too long and may need to be shortened using an extra knot. Note how the sling is girth-hitched to the foot to stop the foot falling out. Note also that the rope is tied back to the harness as a backup.

Jumars attached to the rope with carabiners attached to the top holes to keep the device on the rope even if the gate is accidentally opened.

A **shunt** can be used with double ropes, as shown here. Squeeze the trigger shut to slide up the rope, then release to lock.

A Kleimheist hitch: Tie this like an autoblock but thread an end of the loop through the other end. This works well with webbing, as well as cord.

> **TIP**
>
> The leg loop can be attached to the foot by using a girth hitch or a similar "stirrup" arrangement to stop the foot from sliding out between steps.

attached. A further sling can be used to attach this prusik back to the harness for backup should the top attachment fail for any reason.

Apply tension to the rope by slipping the clutches up the rope as far as they can go, and then alternately pump the leg and waist loops until the rope is fully taut. Stand in the foot loop and slide the waist clutch

as high as it will go. Then relax the leg and hang by the waist, allowing the leg prusik to be slid up as far as possible. Repeat the process. The length of the leg loop should be adjusted so the steps feel comfortable—overstepping is both strenuous and inefficient.

top prusik at least, being relatively easy to slide but locking well when required.

Procedure
Whatever equipment is used, the basic system for rope ascending is the same. (For long free-hanging pitches such as reascending fixed lines on big-walls there are more efficient methods, but these require more equipment or time to set up.)

Attach two clutches to the rope. If you're using prusiks, the top one should be attached to the harness, either directly or using a short sling if the prusik attachment is too tight. The bottom prusik should be long enough to be used as a foot loop—again, this may require a sling to be

A Ropeman attached to a rope: This slides up the rope but locks when pulled downward, like a jumar. However it is awkward to attach to the rope.

Using one leg loop on each jumar: This is an alternative system that can be very efficient if carefully rigged for the climber's dimensions. Note the rope tied back to the harness at intervals to provide a backup.

AVOIDING PROBLEMS

If you progress sensibly through the grades and gain experience on climbs that are not too committing before progressing to more challenging locations such as tidal crags and remote mountain climbs, you are unlikely to run into serious problems. A little forethought can prevent many problems from occurring in the first place.

Communications

Good communication is probably the simplest way to pre-empt potential problems. Discuss a system with your partner that will enable you to keep in touch with each other even when wind or traffic noise drowns out your voices. The usual convention is for the leader to give three sharp tugs in rapid succession when ready to bring up the second climber, with a similar arrangement for replying. The second should use this system carefully, as it is possible to pull the leader off from a precarious move if used at the wrong moment.

Choosing the right belay point

Another important factor in preventing problems is for the leader to arrange the belay in a position where it is possible to see the whole pitch below. This can make an enormous difference, especially when climbing with relatively inexperienced partners who might otherwise climb past protection or miss a traverse point if left to their own devices.

This is particularly useful if the climb has a crux much harder than the rest of the pitch, when a belay situated just beyond will allow a good tight rope to be provided if required, with minimal rope stretch and maximum moral support. Don't feel obliged to continue to the normal stance if you suspect the second will have problems and you find good anchors shortly after the crux. If this is not possible, it may be possible to leave a long sling hanging from a protection point that will allow the second to pull up if the move proves to be too difficult.

Following a traverse can be more intimidating than leading it. Make sure the second is protected by placing protection *after* hard moves.

Here a climber uses long slings on high protection points to **minimize rope drag** as he moves left into a crack system.

Traverses are a common cause of problems for the second climber, but a considerate leader can often arrange for a top-rope to be available most of the time. Tips for achieving this can be found in the *Protecting the Second Climber* section on page 88.

Rope technique

Avoid letting ropes dangle down the rock face where they can snag on spikes or even dislodge boulders when pulled. For rappelling approaches to climbs it is advisable to use a rope bag, or loose coils lapped over the waist that can be fed out as progress is made. If the climb starts from a hanging belay near sea level, it may be possible to uncoil the climbing rope(s) into the rope bag. You should avoid letting the rope fall into the water in any case, because the swell can easily force the rope into crevices, making it difficult, dangerous or even impossible to retrieve.

At belays a little time spent sorting out the ropework can pay dividends later. The aim is to assist the belayer to pay the rope out freely when required. If the same person

Awareness of potential problems is particularly important on climbs with committing approaches such as on sea cliffs.

is leading each pitch, the direction of the rope coils needs to be reversed after the second arrives at the belay. By laying coils on the floor, over a spike or flaked over a belay connection, then working the rope reservoir back toward the lead climber, the lead rope can be paid out smoothly without fear of interruption at a critical moment.

> **TIP**
>
> Time spent training a novice partner how to remove pieces of protection efficiently and how to use a nut tool is never wasted. If some protection is really stuck, though, it is often quicker to get your partner to leave it in place and then climb or rappel down after they reach the belay to retrieve it yourself.

FALLING

The era governed by the adage "the leader never falls" was bypassed with the development of reliable ropes and modern protection equipment. However, falling always involves a degree of risk, and in addition to checking the reliability of the equipment and the belayer, it is worth making an effort to learn how to "fall with style." Make a quick appraisal of the trajectory: if it looks like it will involve colliding with anything solid, then falling is a bad option and you should, if possible, try to climb back down to the last protection

A climber in midair: Notice that a swing will follow as the rope is still following a diagonal line.

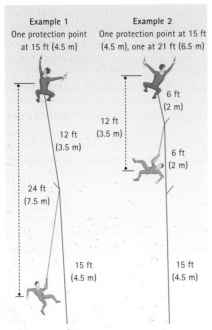

Example 1	Example 2
One protection point at 15 ft (4.5 m)	One protection point at 15 ft (4.5 m), one at 21 ft (6.5 m)

On a climb that will only accept small wires, it is best to place as many as possible. In these two examples the climber has traveled the same distance from the belay, but in the first example will fall heavily onto the one item of protection, as the fall factor is double the amount created in the second example. This creates a much greater impact force on the protection, making it more likely to fail—causing a 54 ft (16.5 m) fall, passing the belayer on the way.

point while your belayer reels in the slack rope. Resist grabbing the protection when you arrive unless it is secure for multi-directional loading, otherwise the gear might pop out and precipitate an even longer fall.

To take control of a fall, push gently away from the rock, bend the knees and arms to absorb any impact, and shield the head with the hands held at about eye level. Fight to remain upright, and don't grab the rope because friction burns are likely to result.

If you really want to master falling techniques, practice them in safety using an overhanging wall with bombproof anchors. Lower to safety, untie from the rope, and retie before taking repeat falls in order to allow the rope to recover. On slabs it may be possible to run back down to avoid grazes, but this is easier said than done.

Basic fall arrest
A skillful belayer can make an enormous difference to a leader's confidence, as well as providing an obvious safety benefit. Practice with a failsafe system: either a second belayer holding the brake end as a backup, or a knot tied in the brake rope a few feet beyond the belayer. Stand directly under the first protection point so that unexpected sideways forces do not catch you unawares.

Dynamic fall arrest

The cushioning effect of rope stretch can be further improved by dynamic belaying, which can actually make the difference between a poor top sling stopping a fall or being ripped out. As the belay device is loaded, deceleration begins. If the rope is allowed to continue running out through the device but is brought to a halt gradually, this significantly decreases the peak impact force. This is fairly easy to achieve with a "slick" belay device but virtually impossible with a "grabbing" device such as a grigri.

Even grabbing devices can be used dynamically by a belayer. One way is simply to jump in the air as the device loads. Alternatively an experienced belayer at ground level can gradually move out from the crag for a better view of the leader. In the event of a fall, as the rope begins to take the load, the belayer walks toward the crag, resulting in a slower deceleration.

> **TIP**
>
> Occasionally, by asking for a little extra rope to be paid out, it may be possible to fall beyond a bulge or roof, and into free space—this requires a cool head.

Ground anchor

Instead of clipping the belayer to an anchor at ground level, the lead rope can be clipped through a low protection point. This should be carefully arranged to withstand the vector force created by the combined upward and outward pull on the rope; a good thread or bolt is ideal for this. To halt a big fall the belayer can significantly reduce the distance by running away from the crag as soon as the leader becomes airborne. This can be combined with stepping toward the crag at the moment of impact as described above, if the leader is not in danger of hitting a ledge.

A short fall is not always better: By paying out some more rope, the falling climber will miss the rock projection. Normally it will be the lead climber that makes the decision whether to pay out or take in rope before a fall.

LOCKING OFF A BELAY DEVICE AND ESCAPING THE SYSTEM

The ability for a belayer to free up both hands is a fundamental starting point for almost any problem situation that cannot be solved by a tight rope or by lowering the climber to the ground. This could be achieved by an escape from the system, meaning that the climber can be left fastened directly to the belay, allowing the belayer to leave the stance if necessary.

Locking off

The most basic problem-solving skill is the ability to lock off the belay device so you can get both hands free. If the person you are helping is actually hanging on the rope, this is essential, unless it is possible to simply lower them to the ledge or to the ground without fear of snagging on a tree or a spike on the way down.

All belay devices can be fastened in the locked position, but some are easier to secure than others. The grigri, for example, is self-fastening once it has locked. Others need to be tied in place, taking care not to let the rope slip while attempting to tie knots. Under the load of a free-hanging heavy climber this can be very difficult.

Tying off a belay plate requires care to prevent fumbling at a critical moment, so it is worth practicing this technique in a safe situation where the rope is loaded but the climber is only a few inches above the ground. Basically, a loop is pushed through the belay carabiner and then locked by pushing another loop through the first loop. This is finished with another half hitch, ideally leaving the live

rope uncluttered with any knots. The locked half hitches should be tied around the back bar of the carabiner rather than the gate.

Releasing the belay device

Practice releasing the device under a load as well because, for example, it may become apparent that the climber can be lowered after all. As you pull each loop free, keep your fingers through the loop so it cannot suddenly slip completely free and catch you unawares.

Escaping the system

Having locked off the plate, the belayer can now connect the casualty or stuck climber directly to the belay anchor, releasing the belayer from the safety system. Ensure that your anchors can take the direction of loading that will ensue. Attach a prusik

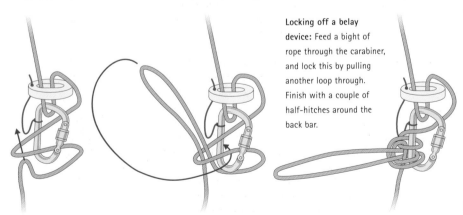

Locking off a belay device: Feed a bight of rope through the carabiner, and lock this by pulling another loop through. Finish with a couple of half-hitches around the back bar.

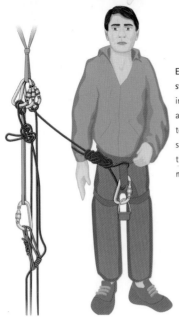

Escaping from the
system: If the belay is
in reach (left) connect
a prusik to the live rope
to the belay using a
sling. Finish by tying off
the rope. Here a Münter
mule has been used.

loop to the live rope using
a reliable prusik hitch such
as a Kleimheist. This can be
connected back to the belay
anchor using a long sling, then
tensioned by sliding the prusik
as far down the live rope as
possible. The belay device can
now be carefully released and
slack paid out to check that
the prusik is holding the load
without slipping. The brake
rope should now be attached
directly to the anchor using
a Münter hitch and removed
from the belay plate. Finally,
tension the rope and tie off
the Münter hitch with a
couple of half hitches.

Anchors out of reach
If the belay is not a
convenient central anchor
point, but is instead one or
two anchors beyond arm's
reach, escaping the system
involves a couple more steps.

Attach a sling to the anchor
ropes using a Kleimheist
hitch and connect this to the
prusik.
  Having escaped the
system, you can secure the
live rope by tying an overhand
knot on a bight below
the Kleimheist hitch and
attaching a Münter mule to
a carabiner clipped into the
loop. The anchors can now
be equalized using slings to
create a central anchor point.
Connect the live rope back to
this and, if necessary, all the
rest of the rope can now be
stripped from the anchors to
be used for a rescue.

Escaping the system with the belay
out of reach (right) involves attaching
a Kleimheist hitch around the rope
or loops that form the belay. This is
treated as a temporary anchor and
the prusik can be attached to it.

RETRIEVABLE RAPPELS AND RESCUE DESCENTS

Retrieving the rope after a rappel

If connecting two ropes, feed the end of one through the anchor point and connect them with a slim profiled knot: the least likely knot to jam on edges is a simple overhand knot. Leave rope tails 2 ft (60 cm) long to prevent the knot from creeping undone under load, but never use a figure-eight knot in this way, as the knot can easily slip off the rope ends when loaded.

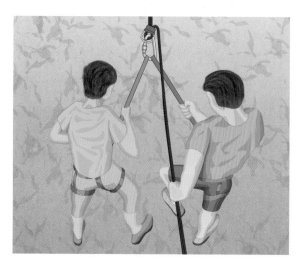

> **TIP**
>
> If in doubt, extend the belay with webbing or cord. Leaving a carabiner behind will drastically reduce friction. The first rappeller can test that the ropes pull freely—just a few inches, though, otherwise you risk heat damage if the rope is threaded through slings.

Rescue descents

On most crags the simplest solution to any significant problem is to use gravity to your advantage by descending. If it is possible to lower a stricken climber back to a ledge or the ground, you should do this as soon as possible to ease their circulation, and then give first aid if necessary. Check first for a clear landing spot.

Assisted rappels: With a conscious person (top), if you have any doubts about the behavior of the casualty, keep the rope on the other side of your body so that it cannot be grabbed by them. With an unconscious person (bottom), it may be necessary to rig a chest harness to help keep them upright and the airway open.

Assisted rappels

If your partner is unable to control a rappel device for themselves, a tandem ("assisted") rappel may be necessary. You can both rappel using individual slings clipped to the same device. Alternatively a long sling can be doubled and tied with an overhand knot to create an inverted Y-shaped lanyard—never rappel with a casualty suspended from your harness, as your body takes the load instead of the rappel device. With this system the rescuer controls the descent, but the rappel device takes the weight of the casualty. Use a prusik backup clipped to your leg loop on the opposite side to your partner.

An assisted rappel may also be the quickest way to rescue an unconscious casualty if the tail end of the rope reaches the ground once you have escaped from the system and attached the casualty's rope directly to the anchor. Make sure the rappel rope is attached to the anchor with a secure knot such as a clove hitch or figure-eight rather than using a Münter mule because these can unzip when loaded on the locking side. Rig the rappel device as above and descend to the casualty, clipping the sling straight into their harness belay loop. Untie them from the rope and continue down the rope together.

Counterbalanced descents

For a rapid escape when your partner has failed to reach the belay, a counterbalanced descent is probably the most efficient means of escape, but only if sharp edges and pendulums can be avoided. After escaping the system, tie the live rope to the belay carabiner using a Münter mule. You can then arrange to rappel on the other end of the rope emerging from the belay carabiner, with a prusik backup attached to your leg loops. It is best to remove the Münter mule at this stage and replace it with a simple loop over the carabiner. The rescuer and the casualty are now suspended on either side of a counterbalance, and the autoblock attached to the live rope to escape from the system can now be carefully removed. You can now descend to the casualty, administer any necessary first aid, and continue the descent by attaching a short sling to the casualty, and thus pulling him or her down at the same time.

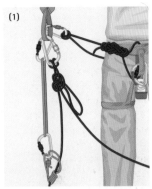

(1)

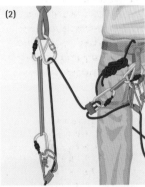

(2)

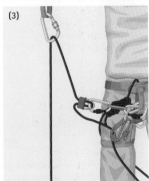

(3)

Setting up a counterbalance rappel:
(1) Escape the system. (2) Pass the rope through a carabiner on the anchor and attach the rappel device to the rope.
(3) Weighting the belay device allows the locking prusik to be removed, and a rappel descent can now commence.

LOWERING AND HOISTING

Simple lowers

If a helpful tug on the rope and shouts of encouragement are not enough to solve a problematic situation, a solution may be found without any need to untie knots or tamper with belays. Unless the start of a climb is tidal, or you approached it by rappel, the simplest evacuation will generally be by descent. Lowering a heavy person down overhanging ground should be approached with caution, however, as it can be surprisingly tiring to keep sufficient grip on the rope, and failure to hold the rope could be catastrophic. Because of this, a backup prusik should be attached to the live rope and linked back to the belay. One hand keeps a grip on this to prevent it from locking onto the rope in normal use, but if control is lost, the prusik automatically grips the rope and prevents it from paying out further.

Considerable mechanical advantage can be gained by passing the rope from the belay device through a high anchor prior to commencing the lower—even better, attach a Münter hitch at this anchor to provide extra friction.

Assisted hoist

By far the most common rescue situation is the second climber requiring assistance to reach the belay—particularly partners attempting a route beyond their normal aspirations. It is a simple matter for a leader who has practiced rescue techniques to effect a 3:1 pulley if the second is less than one-third of a rope length below.

The first step is to lock-off the belay device. An autoblock is now attached to the live side of the rope and clipped into the belay, to act as a one-way clutch.

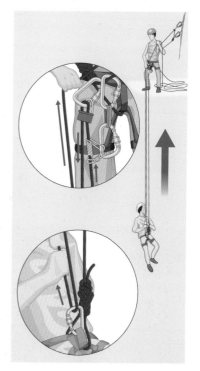

Above: A climber lowers a loop of rope to a stuck partner in order to arrange **an assisted hoist**. Right: An assisted hoist in progress.

A loop of rope with a locking carabiner attached is lowered down to the stricken climber, who is instructed to clip this to the attachment point on their harness. Any slack in the system is now taken in, and the leader is able to release the belay device, which now acts simply as part of a pulley in the hoisting mechanism. The second is able to assist by pulling on the strand of rope traveling toward their harness in the process of hoisting. It is important that the leader keeps an eye on the autoblock clutch system to check that nothing jams up, allowing slack rope to build up with attendant potential for a fall.

Unassisted hoist

Situations can occur where a hoist might be necessary after checking the stricken

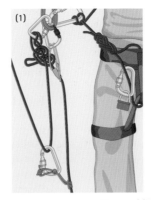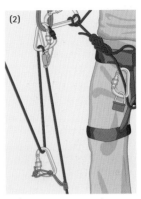

Rigging an unassisted "Z" hoist: (1) The victim hangs from a prusik with a Münter mule. (2) After adding a prusik and making the Z-shape the Münter mule can be removed to start hoisting.

climber's condition—but only if this course of action is less traumatic than a descent, for example, on a sea cliff, or high on a mountain route. The system used is very similar to the assisted hoist, except that instead of lowering a loop and carabiner pulley to the casualty, a prusik is attached to the live rope as far down as the rescuer can reach, and the pulley loop is clipped into this. After raising the casualty a few yards, the prusik will have to be slid back down, away from the belay pulley. It is sometimes possible to use this kind of hoist without escaping the system, but generally the rescuer is too restricted in movement to hoist the casualty effectively.

> **TIP**
>
> When setting up a hoist system, use doubled carabiners or a lightweight pulley to reduce the sharp angles that cause friction.

An unassisted hoist: This belayer has escaped from the system and set up a "Z" hoist, making it much easier to lift his unconscious partner up to the top of the crag.

FIVE COMMON PROBLEMS AND HOW TO SOLVE THEM

1. If the rappel rope jams when you retrieve it

Try to prevent ropes from catching by good planning and observation. Spikes, trees, brambles and so on tend to snag falling rope ends, so choose an anchor above a clear run if you have a choice. Rappel and retrieve the rope on the side of a potential snag. Sometimes you can use a feature such as a groove to keep the rope ends away from obstructions as they fall. Before pulling an end down remember to check you have removed the safety knot from each end.

Don't try to prusik up the ropes if they have snagged while falling: If the rope suddenly releases, it would be catastrophic.

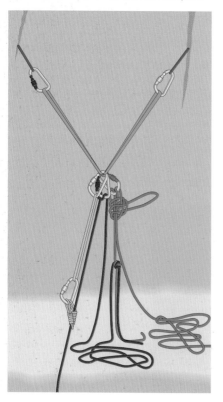

Climb rock back up to the obstruction—you may have pulled enough rope through to be able to use the end of the rope as a lead rope. If you cannot climb the rock, you may have to cut the jammed rope.

2. Passing a knot during a long rappel

If you find yourself having to rappel past a knot, you will need to use skills that are best when practiced a few inches above the ground rather than experimenting above a yawning void.

Set up the rappel and place the backup prusik above the belay device, connected to the harness within arm's reach by a sling. Rappel to within a couple of feet of the connecting knot, lock off the prusik, and attach yourself to a knot in the rope as a backup. Transfer your device to the other rope, lock off the rappel device, and release the prusik. This may be quite difficult; if it's stubborn, use a second prusik to make a foot loop: step up to "un-weight" the jammed prusik and unclip/release it. The foot-loop prusik can then be attached to your harness leg loop as the new autoblock.

3. Lowering past a knot

If you are climbing on double ropes, you may be able to lower somebody all the way to the ground by connecting the ropes. Use a direct belay with an autoblock backup attached to the anchor by a long sling. Lower to within a few inches of the knot and ensure that the prusik has locked. Remove the rope from the direct belay and replace it on the other side of the knot, locking off the belay. Now carefully ease the autoblock toward the anchor until the direct belay is loaded. Remove the autoblock and recommence lowering.

Pre-rigging for a long lower using two ropes connected end to end.

To deal with a climber **stuck on a traverse** you need to either move yourself above them or use the rope to move the climber to a position below you.

On overhanging rock it may not be possible to **lower a fallen leader** to safe ground.

4. Partner fallen from a steep traverse

If a climber falls into space from a steep traverse, lowering may provide a simple solution, or perhaps the climber may be able to prusik back to a protection point. Otherwise you may have to make a controlled pendulum; with double ropes this is normally easy, otherwise you will need to throw some rope to the climber or escape the system and take it over yourself. Attach this rope with a Münter mule, and pay out the other rope slowly to allow a controlled swing until the climber is directly below you and can climb up or be hoisted.

5. Leader fallen and injured

Thankfully this is a rare problem. If you cannot lower the casualty, tie off the ropes at the belay and carefully climb up to the leader. Ensure the top protection point is safe and give any first aid necessary. Create a new high belay and suspend the climber from it with a Münter mule. Now you can carefully strip all the other equipment and make a rescue descent with the victim.

FIRST AID

Serious accidents are thankfully rare for climbers, but a leader fall or dislodged boulder could have serious consequences. These brief notes are no substitute for attending a first-aid course: a complete discussion of current first-aid techniques is outside the scope of this book.

Basic life support

The standard first-aid protocol becomes even more crucial when help is more than a few minutes away. Work through the mnemonic **ABCDE** in order. In an emergency the first three stages of casualty care are urgent.

A: Awareness/Assessment

Appraise the situation carefully—it may be too dangerous to approach the casualty, in which case you should fetch help instead.

Talk to the casualty, and if necessary, squeeze their shoulders and shout to gain their attention. Ask about sources of pain, what happened and if the casualty has any pre-existing medical conditions. Don't forget to call for help.

B: Breathing

A talking casualty is clearly breathing, but if a casualty does not try to communicate,

the most vital task is to check the airway and breathing. Look, listen, feel and smell for signs of breathing. Loosen any tight clothing around the neck, and if no signs of breathing can be felt, the throat should be checked for obstructions. If necessary, tilt the head back carefully to stop the tongue from blocking the airway. Monitor breathing and the level of consciousness every few minutes.

For a nonbreathing casualty the priorities are to obtain help from the emergency services as quickly as possible and to keep the lungs oxygenated through CPR and rescue breathing.

C: Circulation

With a conscious, breathing casualty the priority is to check for major bleeding. Any serious wounds should be immediately treated by applying direct pressure and elevating them, unless other injuries make movement impractical (e.g., an elbow fracture).

If a casualty is breathing and no signs of serious bleeding are found, begin monitoring the pulse as soon as possible in order to evaluate a trend in the vital signs developing over time. Continued rising of the pulse rate for no apparent reason suggests undiscovered injuries or illness.

This unconscious casualty has a head injury and so it is particularly important that blood can drain out of the airway. Despite the cramped conditions between boulders, the first-aider has managed to get him into an approximation of the **safe airway position** and thus kept his airway clear.

D: Deformities: Feel for abnormalities

E: Evaluate, and give Emotional support

Other injuries
Injured limbs
Soft-tissue injuries should be treated as a suspected fracture, requiring immobilization and elevation followed by a visit to a hospital. Splint an injured limb in the most comfortable position, probably using another limb or the chest as the splint. Check that circulation is not impaired.

Exhaustion
Exhaustion leads to the brain becoming poisoned by lack of sugar: many of the signs and symptoms for exhaustion are very similar to intoxication or diabetes, and include withdrawal, irrational behavior, mood swings and bad language. An exhausted climber will gradually lose the ability to spot these signs and fail to take appropriate action.

Cold exhaustion
If cold exhaustion is not dealt with in its early stages, the victim will decline into profound hypothermia, a life-threatening condition often characterized by having too little energy left to shiver. Rescue assistance is urgent in such cases: The casualty must be evacuated with great care on a stretcher.

Heat exhaustion
Regular and sufficient water intake is particularly important in hot conditions so that the body produces enough sweat to cool itself. Heat exhaustion deteriorates into heatstroke if left untreated. A potentially fatal condition that occurs as the body fails to regulate its temperature, heatstroke symptoms include skin that is dry to touch because of lack of sweat production and a full, bounding pulse. Urgent hospitalization is essential.

A helicopter rescue in Verdon Gorge, France. For serious injuries it is generally preferable to arrange a rescue (if possible) than to risk further injuries trying to self-evacuate.

Existing medical conditions
Conditions such as asthma, diabetes and epilepsy do not necessarily preclude people from climbing, but awareness and education are important. Carry extra glucose supplies for diabetics and make sure a climber with a medical condition carries appropriate medication on the route.

153

COMPETITION CLIMBING

Although climbing pits personal ability against the rock face, climbers have always indulged in friendly rivalry, and this was formalized in 1985 with the first climbing competition at Arco, Italy. This was the start of a tradition that has since spread throughout the world.

Types of competition
Most, but by no means all, competitions are held on artificial structures because routes can be created specifically for the event without damaging a natural environment. Of the many types of competition, the main ones are as follows:

- **Bouldering:** Fast-paced events with short routes where several climbers can operate simultaneously on different problems. Usually three attempts are allowed, with diminishing points awarded for success.
- **Difficulty:** Sport climbs led either as a red point after a half-hour's work, beta flashed (see *Sport Climbing* on page 28), or

on sight; official events have routes with a minimum length of about 50 ft (15 m). All pieces of protection have to be clipped, and at appropriate points in the ascent. Competitors are allowed one preview and one attempt at a clean ascent. The height the climber achieves will determine the number of points awarded for the climb.

- **Speed climbing:** Top-ropers compete against the clock to see who can reach the top of the route first—this is arguably the most enjoyable event for audiences.

International competitions
The UIAA is the international sanctioning body through its ICCC (International Council for Competition Climbing) and is composed of representatives from over 60 member countries. The main ranking events are the World Cup—a series of climbing competitions between each country's best climbers—and the World Championship, held every two years. Other international events include

Climbing competitions are usually staged on purpose-built artificial walls like this one, used for the Singapore World Cup in 2006. Eduard Marin Garcia approaches the strenuous overhang.

Bouldering competitions have become an increasingly popular event. Here a female finalist tackles one of several problems on a difficult circuit, attempting to complete each problem "cleanly" at the first attempt.

the Arco Rockmasters invitation event and the Extreme Games in the United States.

Other competitions

These range from informal social events through to official national events for choosing a team. Prizes may be products donated by local sponsors or cash.

Competing in official events

- **Preparation:** Aim to peak at the event by working your training program through cycles until the final two weeks, when it should become specific, e.g., power training for a bouldering competition. Rest for the final few days and load up with carbohydrates, water, and sleep. After the event the first stage of your next training cycle should be recuperation.
- **Your first event:** After waiting in an isolation area prior to competing you will be taken to preview the route for six minutes; this normally gives you a chance to quiz route setters about which wall features can be used and where the boundaries are. The preview allows you to plan resting places, gauge crux sections and visualize moves. Later you will be called to a transition area where the rope

is often attached to your harness. Finally you will be summoned to begin the ascent immediately.

- **Warming up:** Before the climb you should snack lightly on carbohydrates and ensure you are well hydrated. Warm up with light activity followed by slow stretching and some moderate climbing (the holds may give clues about unusual hold types on the route), before resting physically for the final 10 minutes. This is the time to relax and make a final check of your gear to avoid leaving anything in the isolation area.
- **Technical incidents and protests:** Competitions have rules for handling a technical incident or contesting a judge's decision—this covers any situation that causes an unfair disadvantage to a competitor or team, for example, a carabiner that is not set properly for clipping.
- **The climb:** Pace yourself according to the climb, moving fast on steep ground and cautiously on delicate moves. Eliminate any fear of falling and focus on the next move. Never give up without trying the next move, as you will gain points even for just touching the next hold.

ARTIFICIAL CLIMBING

Artificial or aid climbing involves the use of protection equipment to support body weight in order to make progress up a rock face. This ranges from just one or two aid moves while the rest of the pitch is climbed free, to continuous aid climbing for hundreds of yards. Modern climbing aspires to eliminate aid, but some moves may remain aided traditionally if the freed moves are so much harder that they seem out of character with the rest of the route. Some long climbs have pitches that only the strongest teams in the world can climb free; most ascents incorporate at least some aid.

Equipment

Normal protection equipment is used for progress (aid points) with the addition of gear that can only hold body weight, for example micro-cams, thin pitons and various sizes of skyhooks. On climbs requiring piton

GRADING

The original aid grading system (listed here) and its "new wave" variant are used almost universally:

A0   A free climb with an occasional aid move that does not use aiders; pulling on equipment during a free ascent is often referred to as A0

A1   Requires aiders but all placements are solid and easy

A2   Good placements, but sometimes tricky

A3   Many difficult aid moves, and some of the placements might only hold body weight; the risk is still low

A4   Many body-weight placements in a row; the risk is increasing

A5   Enough body-weight placements in a row that a slip might result in a fall of at least 60 ft (18 m)

The new-wave grading system inserts subgradings and accepts a higher level of risk, so that A3+ equates to the old A5.

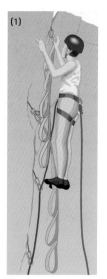 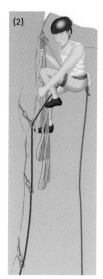

Typical aid sequence using a pair of aiders: (1) Place an aid point and clip an aider into its carabiner. (2) After testing the aider, clip the rope through the top aid point as protection, then transfer to the new high point, moving up to attach your harness with a cow's tail.

placements, a piton hammer is required by both leader and second, but on easier aid climbs pegs are normally left in situ.

Aiders, or etriers, are specialized aid ladders, required for any artificial climb involving more than a move or two. These are essentially super-light ladders made from webbing. They can be improvised using knotted slings, but sewn aiders are easier to use. For easier aiding a pair of five-runged aiders is adequate but for hard aid routes two pairs of seven-runged aiders are desirable. Aiders with metal rungs are also available (but are heavy).

Girth-hitch a daisy chain for each aider to your harness plus a short webbing loop about 10 in (25 cm), with a carabiner or an open hook called a fifi at the other end.

Some climbers carry some wire or even a clipstick to enable long reaches, perhaps past bad rock, but overreliance on these is regarded as cheating.

Typical aid equipment: The cable hanger (top left) is for cinching around metal studs ("rivets") without fixed hangers. A selection of pitons (pegs) are at the top right and near the head of the ax are various skyhooks and a Birdbeak.

> **TIP**
>
> Use thin cord tied or clipped to the eye to prevent dropping the piton if it suddenly works loose.

Method

An organized approach is required to prevent tangles and reduce rope drag. Clip a carabiner or extender into the first aid point (ideally placed at full stretch) and attach your single or paired aider to this. Test the placement by weighting the aider from as low as possible—if a placement fails at this point, it should not involve a fall. "Walk" your feet up the ladder until you can clip the daisy chain into the highest carabiner, and hang from this while planning your next move. It may be possible to stand in the top rungs to allow an exceptionally long reach for the next placement, but this is strenuous and unnecessary for simple placements. Before transferring your weight to the higher placement, clip your rope into the current aid

point as a protection point. After testing you can decide whether to leave it or unclip it, reducing rope drag but risking a longer fall.

Pitons

Placing and removing pitons damages the rocks, so hammerless ascents are preferable wherever possible. Where unavoidable, a variety of pitons is normally carried, ranging from wafer-thin RURPs and Birdbeaks, through blade, lost arrow angle and leper pitons, to bongs, which may span several inches (but have largely been superseded by cams).

Hand-place the piton up to between one third and one-half of its length and then hammer home, ideally right up to the eye. Avoid using holes or butting up against an overhang if you want the second to retrieve it afterward. Placing pitons requires practice and is best done in a disused quarry before embarking on a route requiring pitons.

Seconding

The second can often jumar up a rope to clean the pitch, but sometimes for fun or simplicity it may be preferable to aid climb on a top rope, for example on steep pitches and traverses. Pitons are removed by tapping up and down until they can be eased out.

Steve Mayers on **a difficult aid pitch** on Great Trango Tower, Pakistan.

BIG-WALL CLIMBING

Big walls are enormous rock faces that normally take longer than a day to climb. Nowadays many big-walls have been speed-climbed but this usually requires extensive preparation, or an exceptionally experienced team. Most big-walls are over 2,600 ft (about 800 m) in length, but shorter routes with hard climbing can require big-wall strategies.

Style

A multi-day ascent allows a relaxed atmosphere but requires overnight equipment, so sack hauling will be required for at least some of the pitches. It is often not practical to move the camping equipment every night. Sometimes the distance between ledges is too far to cover in a single day, especially if hauling all the bivouac equipment. The purest solution is to travel light and just sprint for the top, taking minimal gear. This is the most committing solution and may not be practical on difficult or unclimbed terrain.

Another way is the "siege" style, where ropes are attached to enough of the climb to allow a final push to the top to be completed. The third way is a pragmatic compromise known as "capsule" style. From a bivouac spot, the climbing ropes are attached to a high point, perhaps with the addition of some extra rope carried for the purpose. The camp is then moved up to or beyond the top of the ropes and the process is repeated. This style is more committing than siege style as it is not possible to rappel back to the ground and return with ease to the high point at a later date.

For speed ascents (a day or less) meticulous planning is required, with no margin for route-finding errors or slow progress on a pitch. Speed ascents should only be attempted by very experienced climbers and will probably involve a pair of climbers moving simultaneously for at least some sections, normally connected by a rope with a few protection points clipped.

Equipment

This is influenced by the style of ascent. Classic big-wall style requires tough haulbags that allow all the supplies to be winched up by the lead climber. Haulbags are streamlined and hang vertically from straps brought to a single point; the best designs can be easily unpacked, even while suspended. Specialized stoves are normally used, designed to hang from an anchor. If natural ledges are few and far between, portaledges may be required. A portaledge is a toughened camp bed designed to hang from a belay anchor and

Climbers enjoy a portaledge camp on El Capitan, Yosemite, U.S.

Using body weight as **a counterbalance** to haul. For very heavy loads this may require two people.

sometimes covered with a flysheet or even a tent to cope with bad weather. Water is a vital commodity, often carried in reinforced plastic soda bottles with a cord or webbing suspension point.

Method

The basic system is very similar to any other multi-pitch climb. Single or double ropes are used but the leader also trails a haul line (preferably a static rope), which must hang freely down the pitch. This can be used for pulling up extra equipment during the lead, and for hauling bags once the belay has been established. The leader arrives at a belay, ties off the main line, and begins hauling. Once the haulbag has cleared the belay, the second begins to follow the pitch, usually remaining lower than the haulbag to free it if the bag gets jammed in a slot or against a roof.

Hauling

Haulbags can be very heavy, so ratchet pulleys and jumars are normally used to gain mechanical advantage. The leader feeds the haul line through a specialized ratcheted pulley such as a Wallhauler or a Traxion. Alternatively a standard pulley can be used in conjunction with a prusik or jumar as a locking device, but this is much less efficient.

The slack is taken up and then the bag can be pulled, using a jumar clamped to the rope as a handle—this can be rigged as a foot loop to "pump" light loads up using the leg muscles, or more likely clipped to the waist to allow body weight to be used as a counterbalance. A "lower-out" line connecting the haulbag to the second is useful for freeing the bag if it gets stuck at overhang. The leader is attached directly to the belay by a long leash and heaves

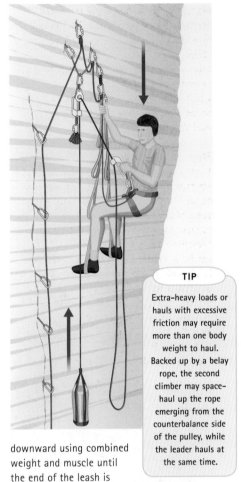

TIP

Extra-heavy loads or hauls with excessive friction may require more than one body weight to haul. Backed up by a belay rope, the second climber may space-haul up the rope emerging from the counterbalance side of the pulley, while the leader hauls at the same time.

downward using combined weight and muscle until the end of the leash is reached, then jumars back up to the anchor to repeat the process. An extreme version of this, sometimes used with body-weight bags for solo ascents, is to rappel down the counterbalance side and jumar up again, hoisting the haul line with one hand as the other pulls up on the jumars. This is known as space-hauling.

Sometimes haulbags just have to be handled along ledge systems, but check to see whether it is possible to rig a hauler further up and organize a controlled pendulum.

BIG-WALL CLIMBING

Aiding

Most big-walls involve some artificial climbing, although this has gradually been eliminated on many pitches by elite parties. For example, Yosemite's most famous big-wall duo, Salathe Wall and The Nose, have both had fast free-ascents, but most teams use considerable amounts of aid and bivouac at least once. Long aid pitches may require up to 50 placements, so equipment must be rationalized, sometimes by back-cleaning part of the pitch by lowering back down from a bombproof protection point, otherwise by stripping intermediate placements on the lead and risking a bigger fall. If the pitch can be clearly viewed, the leader can leave much of the rack at the stance and pull it up from a good placement higher up. You can reduce weight by carrying extension slings to girth hitch onto pitons, but the equipment will still be heavy and therefore a double bandoleer is a sensible acquisition.

It is normally faster for the second to jumar the pitch, tying backup knots as he or she ascends. Many systems are possible but the simplest replaces prusiks with mechanical ascenders, and the foot sling can be effectively replaced with one or two aiders so that both legs can be used.

Left: **A portaledge camp** at mid-height on a new route in Low's Gully, Borneo. The climbers are sorting gear for the day's work.

Right: This climber is learning to **aid climb** by practicing on a top-rope, a safe way to try out difficult placements.

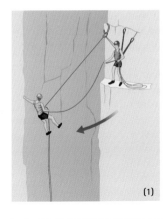

(1)

(2)

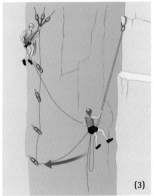

(3)

(4)

A pendulum traverse:
(1) Leader swings out suspended from a high anchor. (2) Lead up the new line. (3) Second rappels from the high anchor and uses tension to move diagonally. (4) Retrieve the rappel rope and complete the pitch.

Pendulums

A single line of weakness rarely breaches an entire wall, so transferring sideways to another crack or groove system is a typical requirement. Sometimes this may be via ledges or a natural line of weakness; otherwise a pendulum may be necessary. This requires an anchor that is higher than the base of the system you want to reach; for example, if the crack is 15 ft (4.5 m) away, your anchor needs to be at least 15 ft (4.5 m) higher. The leader now rappels or is lowered down until enough rope is paid out for the pendulum. The rope is locked and the leader begins to swing sideways. It may be possible to lasso a spike and pull across, or edge

sideways using side pulls (a tension traverse). Otherwise, the leader needs to start running back and forth across the wall until sufficient momentum is gained to lunge for a crack or an edge and begin climbing again. If the climbing is easy, delay leaving any pieces of protection in the new system until the leader is at least as high as the belayer to reduce rope drag, but don't take risks to achieve this.

The second can easily follow a pendulum, provided sufficient rope is available to thread it doubled through the belay anchor. Simply rappel using this doubled rope, then tension sideways using a jumar on the main rope. Once established in the new system the rappel rope can be retrieved.

BEYOND ROCK

A lifetime of fun and adventure can be gained from all types of rock climbing. But bouldering and rock climbing are just specialized aspects of the broader range of activities known as mountaineering. An enormous wealth of experiences opens up to anybody who takes their climbing skills into other territories, but equally, many other safety factors need to be considered. Snow in particular is a very variable medium that can conceal hazards such as crevasses and avalanche conditions.

Ice and mixed climbing

A mantel of snow and ice transforms the cliffs into another world. With spikes called crampons strapped or clipped onto stiff boots and a combination of an ice ax and hammer in your hands, icefalls and buttresses can be climbed in the depths of winter. Leading winter climbs calls for considerable experience because judging the quality of the ice for tool placements is vital. Winter climbing conditions can be fickle—an unseasonal warm spell can strip the ice—but the unpredictability can add to the mystique.

Protection equipment varies according to the type of climb. Icefalls often rely entirely on tubular ice screws, but gullies or snow-covered buttresses (known as mixed climbing) generally require a light rock protection rack, with the addition of a small selection of pitons. Unearthing anchors from the snow can demand both experience and perseverance.

Mountaineering
Scrambling

Scrambles are technically straightforward climbs that tend to follow rocky crests, or to tackle lines of weakness such as gullies that breach an otherwise technical face. Because the climbing is not difficult, minimal equipment is required. On the simplest scrambles little is needed beyond a pair of hiking boots with stiffened soles, plus a rope for retreat or protecting a partner on the occasional tricky section. More complex scrambles can present awkward bulges or airy passages that are strenuous or exposed, and parties may choose to rope up and use belays throughout, so a few slings and a small selection of nuts should be carried. This type of terrain is also often found on sections of very long rock climbs.

The key to fast movement on scrambles is the use of spike anchors and direct belays whenever possible. Although speed is important, it is vital that you thoroughly test the belay before relying upon a single anchor. Scrambles along ridges often require short rappels from pinnacles, so it is advisable to carry a short length of webbing to ease rope retrieval.

Alpinism

As the name suggests, this form of climbing began in the European Alps and then spread throughout the world. Climbing and scrambling on peaks surrounded with snow, or even partly covered with ice, adds a whole new dimension to the sport. Crossing snow patches or glaciers requires extra

Climbing a frozen waterfall (known as an icefall) in Norway. As with rock climbing, slingshot top-roping short routes like this is a relatively safe way to learn.

Climber moving quickly on easy but spectacular terrain on **Aiguille du Tour, Switzerland**.

equipment such as ice axes and crampons to dig into icy surfaces, and the ability to use them. Navigation skills are even more important, as well as awareness of crevasse hazards combined with practice of rescue skills. Sometimes it may be necessary to set up anchors in snow or ice, so buried ice ax belays and placement of ice screws are also important skills.

Many alpine rock climbs are best tackled by leaving the glacier equipment and bivouac gear at the base of the climb and traveling lightweight up the climb, enjoying the mountain scenery. Often the anchors are organized for rappel descents, allowing an efficient party to return to the ground very quickly from any point on the climb. Other routes require the equipment to be carried up the route and may involve a scrambling or glacial descent down another side of the mountain.

Some alpine ascents require ice- and mixed-climbing techniques for sections or even the entire route. This might require quite difficult rock pitches to be climbed wearing mountaineering boots instead of changing into rock shoes.

Super-alpinism

This is the ascent of committing big climbs using alpine or big-wall techniques on remote peaks in areas like Patagonia or the Himalayas. Super-alpinism requires all the component skills and judgments to be thoroughly practiced beforehand. Harder climbs use big-wall siege or capsule style, but modern ascents aspire to forging onward in a style called single-push or pure alpine style.

Louise Turner aiding high up on **Great Trango Tower**, Pakistan. Because of the committing nature of the location, this climb has an official grade of VII.

BOULDER, COLORADO, U.S.

Boulder is a city that has attracted a sizable climbing and general adventure sports community, and the student population ensures a cosmopolitan lifestyle is supported.

The city nestles right under the Flatirons, home to some great climbing only minutes from the city center. The variety of rock types is astounding: granite, various sandstones, quartzite, gneiss and schist locally, with basalt, conglomerate and limestone further afield.

The climbing styles are equally varied. This is a mecca for boulderers, sport climbers and trad climbers with 700 ft (200 m) vertical walls and 2,000 ft (600 m) slabs. The whole area is rich with climbing history and was a focal point in the development of North American climbing for several decades.

Boulder Canyon is another beautiful site with a wide variety of climbing types and beautiful scenery only a few minutes away

from the town. This popular crag consists of highly textured granite, although there are a few areas where the friction is less reliable.

Nearby Eldorado Canyon is one of the world's finest and most famous climbing areas, consisting of beautiful steep fountain-formation sandstone walls towering up to 700 ft (200 m) high. This rock feels more like granite than the soft sandstone found in neighboring states.

These are just the more popular areas. There is a lifetime's exploration to be had here, and that's even without traveling to the neighboring Rocky Mountain National Park.

Getting there

Denver International Airport is less than an hour and a half away. Boulder can be approached by car from just about any direction.

Left: Melissa Griffith tackles the superb "blank rib" of The Sacred and the Profane (5.12d) at **Eldorado Canyon.**

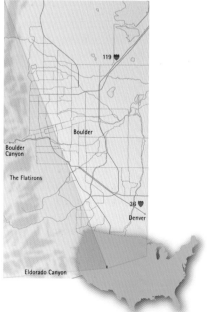

When to go
You can find suitable climbing weather just about year-round, although winter can be chilly. For up-to-date information about temporary access closures during nesting season, check:
www.osmp.org or call (303) 441-3440.

Where to stay
Boulder offers accommodation for most tastes and wallets but there is no cheap camping and the police dish out hefty fines for illegally staying in parking lots.

What to take
A full trad rack or simple set of quickdraws according to your preferred style.

Guidebooks
Rossiter, Richard. *Best of Boulder Climbs.*
    Guilford: Falcon, 1992.
—. *Rock Climbing Boulder Canyon.*
    Guilford: Falcon, 1998.
—. *Rock Climbing Eldorado Canyon.*
    Guilford: Falcon, 2000.
—. *Rock Climbing the Flatirons.*
    Guilford: Falcon, 1999.

Colorado climbing is renowned for steep overhangs presenting boulder problem moves high above the ground.

CLASSIC ROUTES

Climb	Grade	Location
Short routes		
College Drop Out	5.7	Third Flatiron
Avery Ament's Slab	5.8	Flatirons W.C. Fields Pinnacle
West Overhang	5.10d	Flatirons, The Maiden
Arms Bazaar	5.12R	Boulder Canyon, Bell Buttress
Longer routes		
North Face	5.6R	Flatirons, The Maiden
Bastille Crack	5.7	Eldorado Canyon
Super Slab	5.10c/d	Eldorado Canyon, Redgarden Tower One
The Yellow Spur	5.9	Eldorado Canyon, Redgarden Tower One
The Naked Edge	5.11b	Eldorado Canyon North
Vertigo	5.11b	Eldorado Canyon, Redgarden Tower One

RED ROCKS, NEVADA, U.S.

The beautiful mountain and canyon escarpment of Red Rocks lines the Las Vegas skyline and is only a few miles away from the fastest growing and craziest city on the planet. A climbing trip to Red Rocks is always an unforgettable experience.

With its boulders, color-sandwiched walls, canyons and buttresses 3,000 ft (925 m) high, there are thousands of climbs here, with something to suit everybody from novice to hardcore adventure and sport climbers. The rock is sandstone and can be brittle in places, especially after rain. Consequently there are many mixed climbs where bolts are used to bridge the gap between natural placements or to provide rappel anchors for convenient descents. Some multi-pitch routes are bolted throughout but range from safe "clip-ups" to bold run-out adventure experiences. A similar variety can be found in the single-pitch areas near the entrance to the road loop. Limestone crags nearby add yet another huge variety of sport climbing.

The burgeoning metropolis of Las Vegas makes this magnificent wilderness uniquely convenient and accessible. Cheap airfare, nightlife, restaurants, coffee shops and

> ### TIP
>
> The sandstone here feels brittle on first acquaintance and you should certainly avoid climbing for a few days after heavy rain, since the rock is significantly weaker when damp. This is a fragile desert ecosystem and care should be taken to keep to the main trails. This will also minimize damage to your body from the abundant spiky plants.

supermarkets are all only a few minutes away. Crime is a problem in Las Vegas, though, so take sensible precautions with your possessions: Hang on to your wallet and conceal any signs that you may have left your car for the day.

Getting there
Las Vegas's McCarran Airport is the obvious gateway for most visitors, providing cheap and regular flights. Red Rocks is only a few miles west of Las Vegas, but a car is essential for getting around the area.

When to go
Pleasant temperatures can normally be found by seeking sun or shade at almost any time of year, but June through August is often too

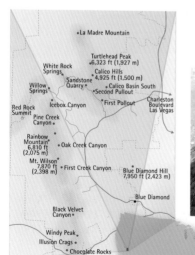

Airy climbing on the third pitch of A Dream of Wild Turkeys (5.10a) on the magnificent **Black Velvet Wall**.

hot for climbing, even in the shade. Although storms are infrequent they can bring strong winds and rain, but Las Vegas has an indoor climbing gym if the weather is unsuitable.

Where to stay
The only campground is the Red Rock Canyon ("13 mile") Campground, on West Charleston (Route 159), 1 mile (1.6 km) from Calico Basin Road. Only large groups can prebook and the sites can fill up during prime season, so staying in Las Vegas becomes the best option if you cannot get a place. It is illegal to stay overnight outside of the campsite without a permit. Contact Red Rocks Canyon Visitor Center: phone (702) 515-5350; Web: www.nv.blm.gov/redrockcanyon.

What to take
Stock up on water at one of the nearby supermarkets on the outskirts of Las Vegas. The approaches and descents are filled with spiky vegetation, so leg and arm cover is recommended. Nights are cold, so a warm sleeping bag, duvet and hat are recommended for campers. A normal light climbing rack, plus about 15 quickdraws, are required for multi-pitch climbs at Red Rocks. Double ropes or a single rope with a thin "tag" line are required for rappel descents. Carry some rappel webbing for less popular routes, but many routes are equipped with bolt anchors with rappel rings.

Guidebooks
Brock, Roxanna. *Las Vegas Limestone*. Fly'n'Carpet Publishing, 2000.
Brock, Roxanna and McMillan, Jared. *Red Rocks Canyon: A Climbing Guide*. Seattle: Mountaineers Books, 2005.
Swain, Todd. *Rock Climbing Red Rocks*. Guilford: Falcon, 2000.

Sport climbing on the beautiful **sandstone** that gives this area its name.

CLASSIC ROUTES

Climb	Grade	Location
Short routes		
Running Amuck	5.10c	Second Pullout
Yak Crack	5.11c	Second Pullout
Running Man	5.11d	Sandstone Quarry
The Gift	5.12c	Second Pullout
Longer routes		
Solar Slab	5.6+	Solar Slab Wall
Crimson Chrysalis	5.8	Cloud Tower
Dark Shadows	5.8	Mescalito North
Epinephrine	5.9	Black Velvet Wall
A Dream of Wild Turkeys	5.10a	Black Velvet Wall
Prince of Darkness	5.10c	Black Velvet Wall
Levitation 29	5.11c	Eagle Wall

YOSEMITE, U.S.

Perhaps the greatest rock-climbing playground in the world, this magnificent park has traditional granite climbs to suit all tastes except beginners'. Yosemite is incomparably beautiful; it is one of the natural wonders of the world, a verdant valley rimmed by 3,000 ft (925 m) rock walls. The style of climbing is characterized by sustained cracks and often run-out slabs, but there are also great opportunities for world-class bouldering.

The magnificent bastion of El Capitan. The Nose route approximates to the line between light and shade.

Getting there

Yosemite National Park is located 200 miles (330 km) east of San Francisco. The most convenient major international airports are Oakland or San Francisco. From either airport a rental car can reach "The Valley" in four to five hours via Highway 120. The journey is possible by public transportation but takes a full day.

When to go

Yosemite is renowned for excellent weather. Because of the wide range of elevations and orientations, good climbing temperatures can be found somewhere throughout the year. Summer cragging is usually uncomfortably hot, but nearby Tuolumne is cooler. Spring and fall are the best times for most routes, and the tail end of the high season (early September) usually gives quiet conditions for a short visit (there are restrictions to prevent permanent residency). Winter can often be too wild and snowy to climb, and storms in late fall can also be dangerously fierce so check the weather forecast before you travel.

Where to stay

Most climbers camp: there is no budget hotel or motel accommodation inside the valley. The famous Camp 4 (Sunnyside Campground) is Yosemite's only walk-in campsite, but each plot is filled until it has six people and there are restrictions on how long you can stay (only a week in high season). For more comfort, and cost, there is the Pines campsite, or there are permanent tents in Curry Village. There is a daily fee for park visitors, and you should follow recommended precautions for storing food safely away from bears. Although there is no town in the valley there are full facilities—a supermarket, cafés and restaurants, plus an excellent climbing equipment shop and medical facilities. Free shuttle buses operate within much of the valley.

What to take

You will require a full trad rack of nuts and slings. Take a double set of cams and throw in one or two larger items as well. Some classic big-walls such as The Nose are climbed hammerless and have adequate bivouac ledges, but most other walls require much more equipment, including pitons, a hammer and portaledges. These massive walls should be attempted only by experienced climbers.

Guidebooks

McNamara, Chris and Sloan, Erik. *Yosemite Big Walls*. South Lake Tahoe: Supertopo, 2005.

Reid, Don. *Yosemite Climbs: Free Climbs*. Guilford: Falcon, 1994.

—. *Yosemite's Select*, Guilford: Chockstone, 1993.

CLASSIC ROUTES

Internet
There are numerous websites but perhaps the most general one is: www.yosemite. national-park.com.

Climb	Grade	Location
Short routes		
La Cosita Left Side	5.7	El Capitan
Bishop's Terrace	5.8	Church Bowl
Lunatic Fringe	5.10c	Reed's Pinnacle
Outer Limits	5.10c	Cookie Cliff
New Dimensions	5.11a	Arch Rock
Longer routes		
Nutcracker	5.8	Manure Pile Buttress
Snake Dike	5.7R	Half Dome
Serenity Crack/		
Sons of Yesterday	5.10d	Royal Arches area
East Buttress	5.10b	El Capitan
North Face Route	5.11c	The Rostrum
Astro Man	5.11c	Washington Column
Big-wall routes		
The Nose	5.9, A2 or 5.13c	El Capitan
Salathé Wall	5.9, A2 or 5.13b	El Capitan
North West Face	5.9, A1 or 5.12	Half Dome

Setting off on one of the world's finest big-wall climbs, **Salathé Wall**, with more than 30 pitches ahead.

SQUAMISH, CANADA

Stawamus Chief is one of the oldest freestanding granite monoliths in the world. It is an area of outstanding beauty, offering long climbs on The Chief, The Squaw, and The Apron, fast-drying single-pitch climbing at the Smoke Bluffs, as well as various sport climbing areas such as Murrin Park, which alone has some 150 pitches. Cheakamus Canyon is also worth a visit for sport climbing, but it is the long trad routes that attract most international visitors.

The 1,800 ft (550 m) Grand Wall is a series of great pitches with highlights being the photogenic Split Pillar (best reached by the Apron Strings/Cruel Shoes combination), The Sword, and Perry's Layback—all unrivaled for position and quality. You should be aware that in the busy season lines are normal on popular routes like The Deidre.

Getting there

Most visitors fly to Vancouver International Airport. From there the easiest access is by car, taking about 90 minutes via the spectacular Highway 99 north to Whistler. It is also possible to catch a Greyhound bus from downtown Vancouver, but getting around at Squamish will prove to be quite difficult without a car.

When to go

The rock-climbing season in Squamish is generally early spring to late fall—earlier warm spells can be dogged by showers.

June through August is the driest season, with daytime temperatures often in the mid-eighties. Long spells of clear, warm weather are typical and therefore provide the best conditions for climbing The Chief's longer walls. From September, the crowds disperse but rain becomes even more likely.

From late November, the winter rains are frequent and, although locals may grab the occasional route, it is a risky time to plan a visit.

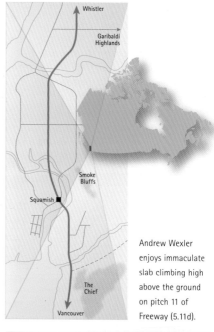

Andrew Wexler enjoys immaculate slab climbing high above the ground on pitch 11 of Freeway (5.11d).

Where to stay

This popular tourist destination has an excellent selection of accommodation options in the area, ranging from very basic camping grounds to luxurious bed and breakfasts. Most climbers use the Stawamus Chief Provincial Park campsite run by the Squamish Rockclimbers Association, which provides water, restrooms, and cooking shelter. This is located on the east side of Highway 99, just north of the Stawamus Chief roadside viewpoint.

What to take

A normal trad rack and double ropes are needed for most of the classic climbs.

Abby Watkins leading the iconic corner known as the **Split Pillar** pitch (5.10b) on one of the world's most photographed climbs, The Grand Wall (5.11a).

CLASSIC ROUTES

Climb	Grade	Location
Short routes		
Klahanie Crack	5.7	Shannon Falls
World's Toughest Milkman	5.8	Murrin Park
Penny Lane	5.9	Smoke Bluffs
Neat and Cool	5.10a	Smoke Bluffs
Exasperator	5.10c	Stawamus Chief
Perspective	5.11a	Murrin Park
No Name Road	5.11b	Murrin Park
Burning Down the Couch	5.11d	Murrin Park
Longer routes		
The Deidre	5.7	The Apron
The Snake	5.9	The Apron
Rock On	5.10a	The Apron
Merci Me	5.8 R	Stawamus Chief
Very long routes		
Ultimate Everything	5.10a	Apron, South Gully
The Squamish Buttress	5.10c	Stawamus Chief
Angel's Crest	5.10c	Stawamus Chief
The Grand Wall	5.11a, A0	Stawamus Chief
Freeway	5.11d	Stawamus Chief

Guidebooks

Bourdon, Marc and Tasaka, Scott. *Squamish Select.* Seattle: Gordon Soules Book Publishers, 2003.
McLane, Kevin. *The Climber's Guide to Squamish.* Squamish: Elaho, 2005.

Internet

See www.drtopo.com for Squamish bouldering and sport climbing topo downloads.

THE ALPS, EUROPE

Regarded as the cradle of rock climbing and mountaineering, the European Alps are one of the most extensive climbing areas in the world. With only 61 peaks over 13,000 ft (4,000 m), they are not as high as the Himalayas or the Andes, but they are very steep with extensive glacial rock. Spanning six countries, the Alps arch from the north of the Italian peninsula via the Julian Alps in Slovenia all the way to eastern Austria, with Germany, Switzerland, and France making up the western border.

With thousands of great climbs and peaks to choose from, the Alps are perfect for rewarding climbing trips or family holidays, offering anything from easy walk-ups to some of the hardest big-wall routes on Earth.

The Alps comprise hundreds of sub-ranges. Broadly speaking, the Western Alps in France and Switzerland are higher and often steeper than the Eastern Alps of Austria and Italy.

Dominated by the Mont Blanc massif, the Chamonix area is famous for excellent granite and gneiss crags throughout, as well as the highest peaks in the Alps. There are 19 sport climbing crags in the Chamonix valley

alone. Up the Rhone valley lies the Bernese Oberland with thousands of alpine routes that take anything from a few hours to a few days to climb.

The Grimsel Pass region features some fantastic sport climbing crags—Sanetsch, Eldorado and Handegg to name a few. There are great multi-pitch granite and limestone climbs and normally ideal weather conditions.

The Italian Dolomites, with the Tre Cime di Lavaredo as its iconic landmark, offer mainly steep dolomite and limestone climbing. The Rosengarten and Sella ranges near Canazei offer great alpine multi-pitch routes that are all within 30 minutes' walking distance from the nearest road.

Getting there
The Dolomites are served by Treviso, Venice and Verona airports. The southern central Alps and Bernese Oberland are best reached via Milan or Geneva airport. Zurich and Bern airports service central Switzerland, and Innsbruck and Salzburg the Austrian Alps.

When to go
Depending on the region and altitude, the season starts in May and finishes at the end of September, but the warmest, snow-free conditions are in July and August.

Where to stay
A vast network of mountain huts (*rifugio* in Italian, *refuges* in French) cater just about every area and peak. They are run mostly by local alpine clubs and give concessions to members of most mountain and alpine clubs.

What to take
You will need a trad rack with at least one set of wires and cams for most longer routes. Larger cams can be useful for Swiss and French granite areas; pure sport climbing crags are nowadays mostly well bolted. Alpine weather can be very unpredictable and at

Granite slab climbing in **Handegg, Switzerland**.

times life-threatening if you are caught high up on the mountain. You will need all-weather clothing and, for big-walls at least, a bivi bag and some emergency rations of food.

Guidebooks

Burnier, Francois. *Crag Climbs in the Chamonix*. Morgex: Vamos, 2001.

James, Ron. *Dolomites, West and East*. Leicester: Cordee, 2002.

Kohler, Annette and Memmel, Norbert. *Classic Dolomite Climbs*. Seattle: Mountaineers Books, 1999.

The **Vajolet Towers** with the famous **SW–Delago arête** (5.4) on the left. Solid dolomite rock and double bolts on all stations make this one of the Dolomites' most enjoyable multi-pitch climbs, although the incredible exposure will get the adrenaline pumping no matter how good the protection.

RECOMMENDED ROUTES AND CRAGS

Climb	Grade	Pitches	Location
Short routes			
Handegg slabs	5.5-10	2-8	Handegg, Grimsel Pass, Switzerland
Sudpilier	5.6	5	Gross Simelistock, Switzerland
Sanetsch, Orphee slabs	5.5-9	4-6	Valais, Switzerland
Delago Tower, SW-Arête	5.4	5	Rosengarten, Dolomites, Italy
Longer routes			
La Luna Nascente	5.10a	9	Val di Mello, Italy
Vinatzer, 3rd Sella Tower	5.5	10	Sella pass, Dolomites, Italy
Motörhead	5.9	16	Eldorad, Grimsel Pass, Switzerland
South face, Aiguille du Midi	5.9	10	Chamonix, France
Cima Grande, NE Ridge	5.5	12	Tre Cime di Lavaredo, Dolomites, Italy
Salbitschiejen, W Ridge	5.8-10	8	Susten Pass, Switzerland

VERDON GORGE, FRANCE

Verdon Gorge is one of the world's great adventure destinations. An exciting rappel from an airy belvedere gains access to stunning climbs perched above a yawning void, basking in Mediterranean sunshine. Huge lammergeyer vultures cruise past like giant relics from prehistory.

The 1,300 ft (400 m) walls are home to routes of all lengths, many of which rapidly gained legendary status and should be on the hit list for any strong team. Because of the rappel access, opportunities for super-long top-rope extravaganzas abound for teams who lack the psyche for leading.

Verdon held center stage throughout the evolution of sport climbing, but as the spotlight has shifted increasingly onto overhanging terrain, its technical slabs, soaring cracks and endless walls have fallen slightly out of fashion. A calm, timeless charm prevails again.

There are over 1,500 routes in this magnificent canyon, ranging from single pitches through to multi-day epic big-walls. Most routes are set in outrageously exposed positions high above the valley floor, and the technical nature of the climbing focuses the eyes upon the feet and the void below. Protection bolts are usually well placed for

The walls of **Verdon's big spaces** tower above the valley floor and the rappel approaches feel truly committing.

tricky moves but often run out elsewhere. It all adds up to an adrenaline-fueled experience.

Getting there
The nearest international airports are Nice and Marseilles. The gorge is not served well by public transportation so having a car is highly recommended, however it is possible to reach the nearest village, La Palud-sur-Verdon by bus from the airports. By car from Nice take the N85 to Castellane, and continue along the D952 for La Palud. From here the climbing in the gorge is less than 6 miles (10 km) away.

When to go
The best climbing seasons are between April and June and from September to the end of October. The sunshine record is excellent and the temperatures are bearable because of the altitude; the plateau is over 3,000 ft (925 m) above sea level and therefore sees plenty of snow in the winter. The summer is often too hot for climbing and the winter is too cold. Should you be caught in bad weather, you could visit the small outdoor, covered training wall in the center of La Palud.

Belvédère di Trescaire

La Polut

Belvédère de la Carelle

Belvédère de L'Escalades

Belvédère de la dent d'Otre

Belvédère du pas de la Baou

Belvédère du Tilleul

Tunnel/Miroir du Fou

Where to stay
The main center is La Palud-sur-Verdon, a delightful village with several campsites. For those wanting a little more comfort there are plenty of *gîtes* on offer around the gorge, including one run by the Club Alpin Français.

What to take
Most routes have good bolt protection, so 12 to 15 quickdraws are a must. You may wish to supplement them by carrying some small nuts. The "classics" demand a normal light climbing rack (i.e., a single set of cams and wires). On old routes it is best to carry a wrench to tighten bolts. For scary leads, carrying a skyhook or two to hook into convenient water solution pockets (gouttes d'eau) may give peace of mind. Most rappel descents are equipped for 165 ft (50 m) double-ropes, and 200 ft (60 m) ropes are often useful. A long rope that is specifically designed for rappelling will not only save time but significantly simplify retreat.

Always carry two prusik loops and use one to back up the rappel. If things go wrong, prusiking may be the only way out.

Pocketed limestone climbing at its best. Mike Weeks top-roping Je Suis une Legende (7a) directly below the **Belvédère de la Carelle**.

Guidebooks
Gorgeon, Bernard and Taupin, Daniel. *Grimper au Verdon*. La-Palud-sur-Verdon: Lie Lagramusas, 2000. Newcombe, Rick. *Rock Climbs in the Verdon: an introduction*. Cumbria: Cicerone Press, 1997.

CLASSIC ROUTES

Climb	Grade	Location
Short routes		
Ctuluh	5.11d	Belvédère de la Carelle
Miroir du Fou	5.11a	Secteur Miroir du Fou
Je Suis une Legende	5.11c	Belvédère de la Carelle
Papy on Sight	5.12c/d	Belvédère de la Carelle
Longer routes		
Voie des Dalles	5.9	Falaise des Malines
La Demande	5.10a	Falaise de l'Escales
Ula	5.10c	Falaise de l'Escales
Eperon Sulime	5.11a or 5.10b, A0	Falaise de l'Escales
Surveiller et Punir	5.11d	Belvédère de l'Escales
L'Ange en Decomposition	5.11c	Falaise de l'Escales
Pichenibule	5.12b or 5.10c, A0	Belvédère de la Carelle

Big-wall routes
These are all on the Paroi Rouge and tend to be very committing and serious undertakings. Get familiar with the Verdon before researching adventures on these esoteric walls.

COSTA BLANCA, SPAIN

The benign climate, excellent transportation links and acres of rock have combined to make the "White Coast" one of the most popular climbing destinations in Europe.

The rock climbing varies from single-pitch roadside crags, through to long multi-pitch sport routes in the mountains and on the coast. There are even some rarely repeated big-wall-style aid extravaganzas. The grades range from beginner's routes through to fierce modern test pieces. Most people visit the area for sport routes but there are plenty of opportunities for trad climbing if you are willing to seek them out.

The showpiece walls of the region are perhaps the Penon d'Ifach and the Puig Campana. The Penon is a vast monolith towering over the popular resort of Calpé. The south face is breached by some fantastic routes—older classics requiring wires and

a few cams, and some excellent fully bolted modern lines. The Puig Campana is an inland mountain with many excellent multi-pitch routes, including the gigantic Espolon Central, which gives 1,200 ft (370 m) of airy but moderate climbing. All these routes require an early start and plenty of water.

Sella is another fantastic base with local accommodation and hundreds of routes at all standards. Although most of the routes are single-pitch, there are sectors with longer routes and some fantastic long traditional routes on the Divino.

Getting there

Nearby Benidorm is one of Europe's most popular resort destinations so regular flights and accommodation can be obtained very cheaply outside the main travel seasons. The nearest international airport is in Alicante, but Malaga is fairly convenient too. A rental car is virtually essential, although it would be possible to spend a week climbing on the Penon or at Sella after reaching the area by public transportation. The A7 autoroute is a toll road that links all the areas and is definitely worth the extra expense.

High above the road on the Via UPSA in the **Mascarat Gorge** near Calpé.

Typical sport climbing in the Costa Blanca. Calpé and the unique Penon d'Ifach can be seen in the background.

When to go

The best time to visit this area is in the cool season, between September and May. The weather is generally at its most reliable in the spring, but this is a popular climbing destination even in the depths of winter.

Where to stay

Accommodation is generally plentiful and cheap in the winter months. Calpé benefits from an excellent central location, and accommodation can be rented from local estate agents. Booking a package tour based at Benidorm is perfectly feasible and a lively but tacky nightlife is guaranteed. There is a climbers' *Refugio* at Sella, right next to the crags, and the Villa Pico in the nearby village is also popular—both can provide pickups from the airport. Camping is pointless except perhaps during busy weeks when accommodation becomes scarce. Another climbers' hostel is the Orange House in Finestrat, but this is not particularly local for crags so a car is required.

What to take

You will want a 200 or 230 ft (60 or 70 m) rope for the sport climbing, and plenty of quickdraws—at least 14. For the longer routes a double rope is highly recommended

CLASSIC ROUTES

Climb	Grade	Location
Short routes		
La Verguenzia II	5.5	Sella
Cefalinpadus	5.10d	Salinas
El Sol	5.10d	Gandia
Starman	5.11c	Forada
The Magic Flute	5.12b	Bernia
Longer routes		
Espolon Central	5.8	Puig Campana
Via UPSA	5.9	Mascarat Gorge
Magical Mystery Tour	5.9a	Sierra de Toix
Via Gomez-Cano	5.10a, A0	Penon
Costa Blanca	5.11b	Penon
El Navigante	5.11c	Penon
Blood on the Rocks	5.11d	Sella
New Dimensions	5.12a	Penon

and some routes require a rappel approach or descent for which a double rope or a separate rappel line are required. Bring a small trad rack if you intend to climb any of the older classics on the Penon or trad routes in places like the Jalon Valley. A helmet is highly recommended for the longer routes (or at least an early start before other climbers).

Guidebooks

Craggs, Chris and James, Alan. *Costa Blanca.* Leicester: Rockfax, 2005.

SARDINIA, ITALY

Sardinia is the second-largest Mediterranean island, measuring about 75 by 168 miles (125 by 280 km). It is packed with crags, mostly various types of limestone, but granite areas can also be found. With over a thousand miles of coastline, there are some fantastic coves and bays with amazing climbing above unspoiled beaches. It is equally suited to a family vacation as a climbing road trip.

The most popular area is the east-coast vacation area centered around Cala Gonone. Here, the multi-pitch Ponoch is an obvious landmark, and the huge Biddiriscottai Cave can be visited by a 20-minute walk north along the coast. The best climbing areas are to the south, around Cala Fuili, which has dozens of routes tucked away in a valley, and the wonderful Cala Luna beach with its tufa-rimmed walls and overhangs. Nearby Dorgali has some excellent pitches, and further west the limestone plateau of Supramonte has some adventurous long climbs including the world-famous Hotel Supramonte (8b).

There are fantastic steep walls around Isili and photogenic granite at Capo Testa, probably best for bouldering and photography.

Concentrated around the town of Iglesias is Sardinia's largest rock-climbing area, with over 600 routes, dominated by Domusnovas with its huge variety of slabs, walls and overhangs demanding all levels of difficulty. The rock climbing here is generally on excellent bolted limestone.

Getting there
The easiest and cheapest way to get to Sardinia for most travelers is by air, though mainland Europe residents often visit by ferry. Alghero is a cheap flight destination. On the island travel by rental car is almost essential, however a flight to Olbia on the east coast allows Cala Gonone to be reached by public transportation, making a week's climbing feasible without a car.

When to go
The best climbing seasons are between late September and the end of November, and then from March to the end of May. Climbing in the winter is also possible, although December to February can be cool and snow can settle on the higher peaks. The summer is very hot and even the sea is warm from May to October.

Sea, sun and rock: Roger Bennion high above an azure sea on the magnificent spire, **Aguglia di Goloritze**.

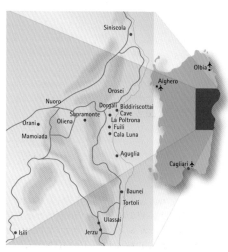

Where to stay

Camping at official sites is a reasonable option in busy periods, but in Cala Gonone the campsite is expensive. Cala Gonone has a small but well-stocked supermarket, but nearby Dorgali has plenty of choice. There are plenty of restaurants, but the cuisine is mainly limited to pasta and pizza.

There are generally plenty of apartments and hotels available in coastal areas, but accommodation can be hard to find inland around Domusnovas, which is not a tourist area. Discreet, free camping seems to be tolerated here, though.

Above Oliena there is an excellent camping spot at the Refuge ENIS Monte Maccione.

What to take

Don't take a rack unless you really want to seek new rock, as this is a sport climbing area. Take a 200 ft (60 m) rope or double ropes for long routes, and 15 quickdraws. Carry plenty of water and sunblock.

Guidebooks

Conca, Corrado. *Arrampicare a Cala Gonon.* Sassari: Edizioni Segnavia, 2006.
> Best guide to Cala Ganone. Available in Italian only.

Oviglia, Maurizio. *Gennargentu, Ultimo Paradiso.* Cagliari: Saredit, 1998.

—. *Pietra di Luna.* Paris: Fabula, 2002.
> Two of the most comprehensive guides to climbing in Sardinia. Published in Italian but available as an English translation.

Internet

There are two English-language, topo-based MiniGuides available on www.rockfax.com, and a very good website dedicated to climbing in Sardinia on www.sardiniaclimbs.com.

CLASSIC ROUTES

Climb	Grade	Location
Short routes		
Guendalina	5.8	La Poltrona
L'eremita	5.10	La Poltrona
Paolina	5.10a	Biddiriscottai
Silvia Baraldini	5.10c	Canneland, Domusnovas
Araj	5.11d	Cala Luna
Wonderland	5.13a	Isili
Longer routes		
Sole Incantatore	5.11a	Aguglia di Goloritze
Deutsch Wall	5.11a	La Poltrona
Wolfgang Gullich	5.11c	Punta Giradilli
Hotel Supramonte	5.13c/d	Gola di Gorropu

The author tackling the crux of the classic tufa and wall climb, **Cappucetto Rosso** (7a) at Cala Fuili.

179

NORTH WALES, U.K.

North Wales is a rugged mountain area renowned for its beautiful green landscape. The whole area is steeped in history and routes like Suicide Wall (E2), Cenotaph Corner (E1), The Bells, The Bells (E7) and Indian Face (E9) set the trad climbing standard of their day both for quality and difficulty.

Of the vast range of outcropping rock types the more extensive rocks include rhyolite, slate, quartzite and limestone. There is an endless variety of venues, with route lengths ranging from roadside single-pitch through to 1,000 ft (300 m) mountain routes.

Although the area is renowned for trad climbing, some world-class sport climbs are located on the north coast around Llandudno and inland at Llangollen, with grades ranging from French 5+ to 9a. Bouldering has recently expanded, but favorites like the Cromlech boulders have been popular for decades.

North Wales has something for everybody. It has some of the best novice trad routes in the world, and also some outrageous adventures that even the most seasoned traveler will never forget. It is no wonder that Plas y Brenin, the National Mountain Centre, can be found in the heart of this region.

You won't need to travel far beyond the park's boundaries to reach other impressive areas. Tremadog on the west coast is a veritable suntrap and rain shadow, while on the northwest tip of Wales, Gogarth is home to one of the world's greatest collection of adventure crags, rearing up to 400 ft (125 m) high from the sea.

Getting there

Manchester Airport is the nearest international airport; it's a two-hour drive from there, but you can drive from Heathrow in about five hours. Public transport is limited in the region, but a shuttle bus service encircles Snowdonia National Park. All things considered, you will get a lot more from your visit by bringing a car.

When to go

The best time to visit North Wales is May and June or September, but the weather can be excellent at any time in the summer if you are lucky. Despite the famously fickle weather, it is possible to climb at Gogarth and the coastal limestone almost any time of year, but avoid rappel approaches in showery conditions.

Where to stay

North Wales is a major tourist destination so there are plenty of places to stay and eat. Llanberis is probably the most central location and offers a full range of accommodation, from bivvies in the slate quarries through camping in Llanberis Pass, to several cheap bed and breakfasts (check out Pete's Eats) and hotels in town. Ogwen is arguably the best center for novice climbers, but

Dave Turnbull on the famous final pitch of **A Dream of White Horses** (HVS 4c).

accommodation is limited to camping or hostels. In colder or wetter conditions, you will get a warm welcome at Eric's Café, where camping, bunkhouses or cottages are available.

What to take
You will need a full rack for traditional climbing in North Wales: A double set of wires and a single set of cams will see you right on most routes. Large cams are rarely needed, but you can find off-widths if you want them. Temperatures are variable so bring versatile clothing and perhaps a light down jacket for belaying in the shade. Waterproof clothing is a sensible precaution for the mountain crags.

Guidebooks
Williams, Paul. *Rock Climbing in Snowdonia*.
    London: Frances Lincoln, 2004.
Panton, Simon. *North Wales Rock*.
    Llanberis: Ground Up Productions, 2006.

Internet
A handy website is www.snowdonia-active.com.

Jack Griiffiths on Left Wall, a world-class classic at E2 5c on **Dinas Cromlech** in Llanberis Pass.

CLASSIC ROUTES

Climb	Grade	Location
Short routes		
The Strand	5.10b	Gogarth, upper tier
Cemetery Gates	5.10a	Dinas Cromlech
Left Wall	5.10b	Dinas Cromlech
Comes the Dervish	5.10c	Llanberis slate quarry
Silly Arête	5.10d	Tremadog, Bwlch y Moch
Stroll On	5.11a	Clogwyn y Grochan
Warpath	5.11a	Rhoscolyn
Axle Attack	5.11c	Pen Trwyn
Longer routes		
Grooved Arête	5.4	Tryfan, east face
Tennis shoe	5.7	Idwal Slabs, Ogwen
A Dream of White Horses	5.8	Gogarth, Wen slab
White Slab	5.10a or 5.9, A0	Clogwyn du'r Arddu (Cloggy)
Vector	5.10b	Tremadog, Bwlch y Moch
The Moon	5.10c	Gogarth, Yellow Wall
Positron	5.11b	Gogarth, main cliff

ARAPILES, AUSTRALIA

Arapiles (Djurid) houses 2,000 quality routes, condensed into one small mountain, up to about 500 ft (150 m) in height. It has been described by many as the finest crag on the planet. The exceptionally tough sandstone supplies plentiful solid nut placements, so most routes are traditionally protected. There are some bolted routes, but even these feel adventurous because few have fixed hangers, requiring a bolt plate

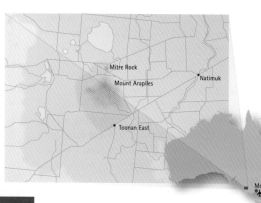

or wire to be placed over the head. There is something for everybody here, from fine beginner's climbs to some of the world's hardest pitches.

Getting there
The nearest international airport is in Melbourne, where you can rent a car and drive for five hours or take public transportation—train to Ballarat then bus to Horsham. Once established at the Arapiles you don't really need a car. Supplies can be picked up in Horsham, about 20 miles (32 km) away.

When to go
The summer period is between November and April. Climbing is possible year-round but seek out the shade in the summer. The routes can get very busy during the Easter vacation. In the winter some lines are sheltered from rain and can usually be climbed (e.g., Oceanoid, grade 5.9).

Where to stay
The local climbers' bar is in nearby Natimuk. Most climbers camp at one of three official campsites (the biggest is the Pines), all situated at the foot of the crags, with environmentally friendly toilet facilities, drinking water, and a public telephone, but little else. Wood fires are not allowed during the summer.

The author climbing on Bard Buttress at **Arapiles**.

The author indulging in some wide stemming on the classic corner line of **Orestes** (5.11c). In the midday sun this proved to be quite a struggle.

If you find Arapiles to be too crowded and dusty for your taste, you can drive to the Grampians. With thousands of incredible climbs, the Grampians would enter this world-climbing gazette if it were not for the proximity of so many easy-access climbs at Arapiles.

What to take

A full trad rack, plus a few "bolt plates," which you can buy from any Australian climbing shop (the nearest is at Natimuk) or you may be able to borrow some from a local. You can generally get by with a single rope, but double ropes are recommended for wandering lines. You will need full camping equipment, including perhaps a spare storage tent, a table, and chairs for comfort.

CLASSIC ROUTES

Climb	Grade	Location
Short routes		
D. Major	5.6	Organ Pipes
D. Minor	5.8	Organ Pipes
Muldoon	5.8	The Atridae
Missing Link	5.9	The Bluffs
Tannin	5.10b	Organ Pipes
Thunder Crack	5.10c	The Bluffs
Kachoong	5.11a	Northern Group
Orestes	5.11c	The Atridae
Dispatched	5.11d	The Bluffs
Punks in the Gym	5.14a	The Pharos
Longer routes		
Tip Toe Ridge	5.1	Pinnacle Face
The Bard	5.7	Bard Buttress
Watchtower Crack	5.8	Watchtower Face
Eurydice	5.10a	Bard Buttress

Guidebooks

Mentz, Simon and Tempest, Glenn. *Arapiles Selected Climbs.* Moonee Ponds: Open Spaces Publishing, 2001.

—. *Grampians Selected Climbs.* Moonee Ponds: Open Spaces Publishing, 2001.

Internet

A good starting point is www.chockstone.org.

CLIMBING DEVELOPMENT

Qualifications and careers

Earning a living from your hobby is a concept that many dream of but unfortunately few achieve. Climbing is not a heavily sponsored sport so there are no really lucrative deals for talented athletes. There is currently little interest in televising climbing competitions, so even the winnings from major international events would not be enough to finance a sporting career with a healthy exit plan into early retirement. The most successful competitors, however, do earn enough money to make a reasonable living while they are at the top of their game.

Exceptionally talented climbers operating at the highest standards of the day might attract sufficient media attention that equipment manufacturers will consider a sponsorship deal; this rarely extends far beyond free equipment and a flat fee for every published photograph and interview. Again, this can provide enough cash to get by while the climber is performing at the highest standard of the day, and is willing and able to stay in the limelight. This requires a flair and desire for self-promotion. The lecture circuit can supplement income with a good agent and an entertaining stage presence. Writing for magazines, books or the Internet can provide additional income but the prestige reward is considerably higher than any financial gains.

The author climbing in Italy. An International Mountain Guide and climbing coach, **Steve Long** is the chief officer for the U.K. Mountain Leader Training Board and chairman of the UIAA Training Standards Group.

Industries associated with climbing provide career openings, such as developing and testing clothing and equipment, plus marketing and sales. Many climbers work in catering or building industries to live close to climbs and fund their activities. Climbing skills are still in high demand for roped access work as an alternative to scaffolding, generally requiring membership of an organization such as the U.K.-based Industrial Roped Access Trade Association, requiring specialized training and assessment plus engineering abilities. TV and movie safety work can offer rare but lucrative opportunities requiring similar skills.

This brings us full circle to instructors, coaches and guides, a group of climbers described in one of the opening sections of this book. Although not many countries require instructors or coaches—whether voluntary or professional—to hold formal qualifications, external training and assessment have the benefit that they allow a thorough grounding in many professional issues that may be missed by a self-taught approach. They also provide professional support and guaranteed insurance cover for both teacher and students.

Becoming a fully qualified teacher or guide is a long and demanding process, and once qualified there is considerable competition for work. Patience, continuing professional development (including first-aid revalidation), good market awareness, networking, and a flexible approach are all vital for success in this rewarding career path.

Contacts
U.S. Instructors/guides: www.amga.com
Canada Instructors: www.eneq.org; guides: www.acmg.ca
U.K. Instructors/coaches: www.mltuk.org; guides: www.bmg.org.uk
Australia Instructors: www.acia.com.au
South Africa Instructors: www.mdt.za.org

Further reading
Cox, Steven M. and Fulsaas, Kris, eds. *Mountaineering: The Freedom of the Hills* (7th ed.). Seattle: Mountaineers Books, 2003.
Fyffe, Allen and Peter, Iain. *Handbook of Climbing*. London: Pelham, 1990.
Goddard, Dale and Neumann, Udo. *Performance Rock Climbing*. Mechanicsburg: Stackpole Books, 1994.
Hattingh, Garth. *Extreme Rock and Ice: 25 of the World's Greatest Climbs*. London: New Holland, 2000.
Houston, Mark and Cosley, Kathy. *Alpine Climbing: Techniques to Take You Higher*. Seattle: Mountaineers Books, 2004.
Horst, Eric. *Training for Climbing: The Definitive Guide to Improving your Climbing Performance*. Guilford: Falcon, 2002.
Libby, Peter. *Rock Climbing*. Capel Curig: MLTUK, 2004.
Long, John and Luebben, Craig. *How to Rock Climb: Advanced Rock Climbing*. Guilford: Falcon, 1997.
Lowe, Jeff. *Ice World: Techniques and Experiences of Modern Ice Climbing*. Seattle: Mountaineers Books, 1996.
Ogden, Jared. *Big Wall Climbing: Elite Technique*. Seattle: Mountaineers Books, 2005.
Shepherd, Nigel. *The Complete Guide to Rope Techniques: A Comprehensive Handbook for Climbers*. Guilford: Lyons Press, 2002.
Tyson, Andy and Loomis, Molly. *Climbing Self Rescue: Improvising Solutions for Serious Situations*. Seattle: Mountaineers Books, 2006.

Further viewing
Self Rescue for Climbers, Olly Sanders and Steve Long, Rock and Sea Productions, 2006.
Stone Monkey, Johnny Dawes and Alun Hughes, Alun Hughes Productions, 2006.
Hard Grit, Rich Heap and Mark Turnbull, Slackjaw Film, 2006.
Return 2 Sender, Peter Mortimer, Axolot Productions, 2004.

GLOSSARY

Adventure climbing: *see* Traditional (trad) climbing

Aiding/aid climbing: A form of rock climbing that requires artificial assistance, i.e., pulling up on equipment to ascend.

Aider: A type of ladder used for aid climbing. Also called an *étrier*.

Aid points: Gear attached to the rock from which to hang when aid climbing.

Anchor: A failsafe attachment point for protection.

Arête: A sharp edge, either vertical or horizontal.

Arm bar: A forearm jammed across a wide crack using a camming effect in order to make progress.

Artificial climbing: *see* Aiding/aid climbing

Autoblock: A prusik used as a one-way clutch or pulley. Also known as a French prusik or "Machard" prusik.

Back-cleaning: Removing protection you no longer have use for as you progress along a pitch.

Barn-door: Term for the way the body can swing out from the rock—like a barn door.

Belay device: A mechanical device used when belaying.

Belaying: The act of protecting a climber from falling by using a rope.

Beta: Information on how to successfully complete a particular climbing route.

Bombproof: A totally secure protection point or belay. Also known as a bomber.

Bouldering: Climbing on boulders near the ground. Usually unroped.

Cam: Rotational effect allowing a limb or anchor device to jam more securely when pulled downward. Principle used in spring-loaded camming devices.

Clipstick: A telescopic device for attaching a quickdraw to a high first bolt.

Commitment, level of: A term used to define how hard a climb is.

Cow's tail: A sling girth-hitched onto the harness attachment point.

Crank: *(slang)* To pull on a hold as hard as possible.

Crimp: A small but positive hold or the process of pulling on a crimp.

Crux: The most difficult section of a climb.

Deadpoint: The apex of an upward dynamic move or leap.

Dynamic rope: A rope that stretches to absorb impact, vital for lead climbing.

Dyno: A lunge or leap to grab a hold.

Edging: Using the edge of a climbing shoe on a small foothold.

Escaping the system: Transferring the weight of a hanging climber directly to the anchor, so that the belayer can move away to solve a problem.

Étrier: Another name for an aider.

Extender: *see* Quickdraw

Face climbing: Ascent of a rock face rather than cracks or chimneys .

Fifi: A metal hook shaped like a question mark that is used for aid climbing.

Fixed gear or fixed equipment: Equipment that is left in place for subsequent climbers. Usually a bolt, peg, or threaded webbing.

Flake: A thin slab of rock detached from the main face.

Gaston: A technique that involves pulling to the side with the elbow pointing out and the thumb down. Named after the French climber, Gaston Rébuffat.

Gouttes d'eau: Pockets in the rock caused by water erosion.

Grade: An approximate measure of the technical difficulty of a climb.

G-Tox: A method of shaking out the arms which utilizes gravity to shorten muscle recovery time.

Hangdog: Hanging on the rope or an anchor for a rest. Known as "dogging."

Hanging belay: The end of a pitch with anchors but no ledge.

Impact force: The maximum force affecting the climber and anchors as a falling climber is brought to a halt. The faster the deceleration, the greater the impact force.

Kleimheist hitch: A versatile prusik hitch that can be tied using cord or webbing.

Knee bar: Similar to an arm bar but using either the thigh bone or the lower leg cammed across a wide crack.

Knee lock: The knee joint inserted into a crack and then jammed by bending the knee. Can be difficult to release.

Lead climbing: Belayed climbing where the lead climber trails the rope and clips the belay rope through anchors to reduce the length of potential falls.

Left-right diagonal: Combination of, for example, right hand and left foot on holds to give a strong braced position through body tension. Particularly effective on steep rock.

Off-width: A crack that is too wide for effective hand or foot jams but too narrow to chimney.

Pitch: The portion of a climb between two belay stations.

Protection/protection equipment: The name for equipment that is attached to the rock in order to enable climbing. If the equipment is placed by hand rather than hammered into the rock, this is normally called natural protection.

Quickdraw: A sling with a carabiner at each end, used to reduce friction when attaching the belay rope to protection equipment. Also called an extender.

Rack: The set of protection equipment used for a climb.

Redpoint: To complete a lead climb without falling or resting on the rope, after prior practice.

Ripples: Undulations in a slab surface that may allow the feet to gain a hold through friction.

Roof: A substantial horizontal overhang.

RP: A specialized brass micro-nut manufactured in Australia.

Run out: A climb that requires the lead climber to move a long way above any protection. You don't want to fall!

RURPs: Tiny postage-stamp-sized blades used as fixed equipment—Realized Ultimate Reality Pitons.

Sharp end: *(slang)* The lead (top) end of a rope when lead climbing.

Slab: An inclined sheet of rock—normally featureless with few holds.

SLCD: Abbreviation for Spring-Loaded Camming Device—a mechanical protection device that is often simply called a cam.

Sling: Webbing (tape) sewn or tied into a loop. Also called a runner.

Smearing: Relying entirely on friction for footholds, in the absence of any positive edges.

Sport climbing: Climbs with reliable protection points left permanently in place (in situ, or fixed gear).

Spotting: A way of reducing the hazard for unroped climbers. One person or several people shield a climber from a bad landing with their hands.

START: A simple way to create a safe belay—Simple, Tested, Angle, Reliance, Tensioned.

Static move: A slow reach for a hold, the opposite of a dynamic move which involves "slapping" or even jumping for a hold.

Static rope: A nonelastic rope, useful for situations other than lead climbing.

Sticht plate: A belay device consisting of a flat plate with a single or, more commonly, a pair of slots, often used generically.

Topo: A diagrammatic plan of a climbing route.

Traditional (trad) climbing: Climbing that is protected mainly or entirely by equipment carried and placed by the lead climber.

Undercling/undercut: A hold/flake that faces downward. Also used as a verb.

Weighting (the rope): Resting by hanging on the belay rope. Not allowed in a clean ascent.

INDEX

INDEX

INDEX

ACKNOWLEDGMENTS

Special thanks to Rachel Kelsey, Marcus Daws, Gavin Lim, Wendy Yuen (the models) and all staff at The Third Space and The Castle Climbing Centre in London for the use of their climbing walls, Snow and Rock for supplying equipment for the photo shoots, Five Ten, Black Diamond, Lyon Equipment, and Cathy at Mountain Works for all her invaluable assistance.

The author would also like to thank his long-suffering wife and the Mountain Training Trust (Plas y Brenin).

Illustrations by Mark Franklin (pages 36, 39 & 46 by Nick Tibbott)

Photographs
Getty Images 8, 9t; Chris Bonington Picture Library 9b, 10, 12, 13t, 15; Knut Burgdorf 1, 2–3, 6, 30a, 90r, 91b, 96b, 98l, 106, 111tl, 167, 172, 173. Steve Gorton 11, 16, 102l, 104t, 109tc, 109tr, 117, 119, 122, 181; Roland Marloh 90l, 108t; © René Robert 13b; Steve Long 18, 19, 24t, 25, 33l, 44, 56, 57t, 63, 65, 71, 73, 75, 77r, 79, 80, 81, 85, 88, 91tl, 102r, 103, 105tr, 116t, 124, 128, 133, 140, 151r, 152, 153, 155, 157b, 158, 160, 163, 166, 168. 169, 174, 175, 176, 177, 178, 179, 180, 182, 183, 184; Wolf Marloh 26, 27t, 67br, 109br, 134, 143; Mountain Works/Tim Glasby 20, 32; Kelsey Adventures 24, 27r, 28, 30, 31, 61, 105tl, 130, 131, 132, 141r, 142, 151l, 162; Corbis 33r, 96t, 101; Mountain Works/Zero-G 34t, 35c, 38t, 40t, 42, 45bl; courtesy of Five Ten 37; Black Diamond 38b, 39, 49r, 157t; Petzl 47; Mountain Works/Paul Casey 107; © Action Plus 114; Mountain Works/Craig Hiller 115; John Dunne archive 126t; © David Simmonite 126b, 127; Angela Goodacre Donini 129; © Action Images 141l, 154; © Simon Carter/Onsight Photography 164, 170, 171; © Greg Epperson 165.

All other photography by John Freeman